D1522071

A Defense of Ignorance

A Defense of Ignorance

A Defense of Ignorance

Its Value for Knowers and Roles in Feminist and Social Epistemologies

Cynthia Townley

LEXINGTON BOOKS
A division of
ROWMAN & LITTLEFIELD PUBLISHERS, INC.
Lanham • Boulder • New York • Toronto • Plymouth, UK

Published by Lexington Books
A wholly owned subsidiary of The Rowman & Littlefield Publishing Group, Inc.
4501 Forbes Boulevard, Suite 200, Lanham, Maryland 20706
www.lexingtonbooks.com

Estover Road, Plymouth PL6 7PY, United Kingdom

British Library Cataloguing in Publication Information Available

Library of Congress Cataloging-in-Publication Data
Townley, Cynthia.
  A defense of ignorance : its value for knowers and roles in feminist and social epistemologies / Cynthia Townley.
     p. cm.
  Includes bibliographical references.
  ISBN 978-0-7391-5105-1 (cloth : alk. paper) — ISBN 978-0-7391-6818-9 (ebook)
  1. Feminist theory. 2. Ignorance (Theory of knowledge) 3. Social epistemology. I. Title.
  HQ1190.T69 2011
  305.4201—dc22   2011009702

Contents

Preface

The ideas for this book originated as my PhD dissertation, completed in 2000 at the University of Tasmania, and sparked by the idea that ignorance had a more important role in epistemology than had been recognized. Ignorance seemed to show up only as the specter of skepticism or as some kind of failure to achieve knowledge, but I set out to explore whether ignorance could have more interesting and possibly more valuable roles. The field of epistemology has expanded since then, and connections to other discussions of ignorance, social epistemology, epistemic virtue, and epistemic justice have become evident. I hope that this book will now be useful to others working in the neighborhood of these ideas.

I am grateful to many people for supporting this project in its various stages. I especially thank my thesis supervisors Marguerite La Caze and Jay Garfield without whom I could not have turned my initial ideas into the work that started this project. My graduate student colleagues in the philosophy department at the University of Tasmania where I completed the PhD provided extensive moral and intellectual support, and an exemplary philosophical community during that first phase.

My thinking has benefited from generous comments by the external examiners of the dissertation, and more recently from constructive reports from anonymous reviewers. Jay Garfield and Mitch Parsell have commented extensively on various versions and provided invaluable encouragement along the way. I am deeply indebted to those critical friends. Macquarie University supported sabbatical time in 2006 and 2010, members of the Philosophy Department at Smith College were gracious and generous hosts in 2006, and my colleagues in the Philosophy Dept at Macquarie University provide an exceptional intellectual environment in which to think and work. Mary

Walker's assistance with preparing the final manuscript was invaluable, and I am privileged that my friend Brett Salter created the image for the cover.

If this work has any strengths, they are due to what I have learned in and from my philosophical communities. Without them I could not have done this work. Its flaws are all my own.

Introduction: Ignorance Matters

Ignorance matters because as epistemic agents interact with one another and we share information, as theorists and as people concerned with knowledge, we are in fact dealing with ignorance as much as with knowledge. Yet until recently, philosophers interested in knowledge have paid little attention to ignorance.[1] Epistemologists have tended to ignore ignorance, in contrast to the attention paid by ethicists to various forms of evil. Most epistemologists have assumed that acquiring knowledge, supplemented with sharing knowledge in accounts of testimony and in social epistemology, is the central epistemic goal.[2] When epistemic dependence is considered, the ideal and virtuous knower is maximally informed and maximally informative, so the elimination of ignorance remains an uncontroversial good. I will show that ignorance, far from being an epistemic flaw always in need of remedy, is demanded by some of the epistemic virtues that a responsible epistemic agent (understood as a social agent) needs to possess. Epistemic value comprises more than knowledge and what leads to knowledge.[3] It is simply false that, from an epistemological point of view, it is always desirable to reduce ignorance. Ignorance has a variety of forms and functions, and not all are negative.

We cannot understand a wide range of epistemic practices solely as practices devoted to increasing knowledge. Trust, empathy, discretion, and discrimination all demand forbearing to seek or to share information, and maintaining one's own or another's ignorance in some way. Since these practices are not always subordinate to a goal of increasing (acquiring or sharing) knowledge, to understand these activities as valuable, we need epistemic standards that account for, even accommodate ignorance, not ideals that require it to be reduced or eliminated. Ideals that entail the elimination of ignorance don't set the standards for agents such as ourselves to be doing well with knowledge. They set up a distorted picture of epistemic virtue that presents certain activities in an excessively positive light, and others in an excessively negative one. Thus, there are practical and theoretical imperatives to revise epistemology so that it attends to ignorance.

This book defends three interrelated claims: 1. That understanding relationships is integral to understanding epistemic practices; 2. That epistemic values are not reducible to the value of increasing knowledge; and 3. That ignorance is not merely inescapable for epistemic agents, but is valuable. Much traditional epistemological discussion (perhaps most discussion in analytic epistemology) takes for granted not only that increasing knowledge is the definitive epistemic goal, but also that independent means of acquiring knowledge are superior to those involving dependence. Since my project challenges these assumptions, it is an exercise in revisionary epistemology, although it is also part of the expanding fields of social epistemology and feminist epistemology.[4] An adequate epistemology must pay attention to epistemic interactions, both for theoretical completeness, and in order to be useful, since most dealings with knowledge are dealings with other knowers.[5] Epistemology must address epistemic dependence, and I demonstrate that it must therefore attend to ignorance. While it may seem surprising that any form of ignorance can be an epistemic good, ignorance is practically indispensable for a community of knowers and an account of ignorance is theoretically necessary for an adequate epistemology.

Ignorance has at least the following forms, which are not mutually exclusive. First, ignorance can be a lack of knowledge or information that could be acquired relatively simply, by, for example, observing or asking. I call this simple ignorance. Second, there can be entrenched, interested and invested ignorance exemplified in Charles Mills' work on epistemologies of ignorance in *The Racial Contract*.[6] Here, ignorance is systematically produced and sustained, to misrepresent reality in ways that not coincidentally sustain patterns of racial privilege. Invested ignorance includes ignorance of one's own privilege, and can both support and be reinforced by a misguided sense of merit or superiority. Miranda Fricker's hermeneutic epistemic injustice can involve a similar form of ignorance. She describes cases in which a "hermeneutical lacuna" prevents an understanding of a distinct social experience, such as sexual harassment, before the label and description were developed.[7] Arguably those who gain some kind of satisfaction from indulging in sexually harassing behaviors have invested ignorance in the conditions that permit this indulgence. Invested ignorance can also be seen in the tendency of medical practitioners to succumb to cultivation by medical device and pharmaceutical companies. Practitioners may sincerely believe they are unaffected by these relationships, but evidence suggests otherwise.[8] The widespread tendencies to ignore the evidence of the effects of both generous and small gifts on prescribing practices and to deny that I (unlike others) could be influenced by such gifts are manifestations of invested ignorance.

A third kind of ignorance (a counterpart to some varieties of invested ignorance, such as the ignorance of racial privilege), is a view of members of some group as characteristically ignorant, not merely lacking some information, but fixed in some inferior condition, such as lacking a capacity for a rational or objective view, a sophisticated understanding, or a civilized perspective.[9] Related, but distinct, is the recognition by one group that another group is systematically ignorant. This can describe the way that members of a subordinate group respond to the ignorance of the privileged group, by exploiting the opportunities this offers for subversion. Pharmaceutical marketers might also trade on the invested ignorance of medical prescribers—the marketers know what kinds of interventions increase their sales, but the prescribers might not be aware of the extent and type of changes to their choice to recommend certain medications. These are forms of ascribed and applied ignorance. A further category includes the ignorance that accompanies selectivity—inevitably, pursuing one kind of inquiry can leave another in the background. Such neglect can become problematically embedded in some disciplines, as Sandra Harding explains in relation to philosophy.[10]

My discussion is mainly concerned to explore the first and simplest kind of ignorance, and to point out where it can be valuable. I begin with simple ignorance in order to develop an epistemology that takes it seriously, and which is both sensitive to relationships with other forms of ignorance, and can engage with the work that explores them. Less attention has been paid to simple ignorance than to invested, applied and ascribed ignorance. This is mainly because explorations of ignorance have emerged not from mainstream epistemology, but from identifying how ignorance can function in patterns of social organization along class, race, and gender lines, and its presence in patterns of discovery and authentication in science.

Current attention to ignorance comes from a range of historic, sociological, and political disciplines, often prompted by concerns about social privilege, and to uncover practices of "systemic unknowing."[11] Feminists, race theorists, and post colonial theorists have been actively exploring the importance of ignorance in shaping the social world, recognizing that ignorance itself is complex, and, for example, operates both as a mechanism of oppression and of strategic resistance.[12] To some extent, considering ignorance "from an epistemological point of view" is artificial, as no human being is a pure epistemic agent; all our knowledge practices are socially situated, motivated by, and grounded in our complex and concrete lives. However, it is important to engage with philosophy of knowledge on its own terms, and doing so involves a degree of abstraction and generalization. The result of this engagement is not only a revision of some longstanding assumptions within epistemology, but also an analysis of some dimensions of epistemic interdependence that will be useful in more practical contexts.

While I reject the global imperative to eliminate ignorance, I do not deny that there are cases when ignorance should be remedied. False claims to knowledge, and denial of ignorance in the face of reasons to acknowledge it, are problems both on my account and on traditional accounts, and likewise for the mis-ascription of ignorance, or denial of knowledge to others (often as part of other mechanisms of unjust dismissal or subordination). I touch on some of these issues briefly in what follows, but the main concern of the book is to uncover and defend the presence of ignorance, in oneself or in another, where there is no epistemic imperative to remedy it, and good epistemic reasons not to do so. That is to say, I defend an epistemology in which ignorance can be viewed positively, neutrally, or negatively, in contrast to standard views in which a positive attitude to ignorance is not an option. Because the standard attitude to ignorance is negative, my discussion aims to show where this should be revised. Revealing ways in which ignorance can be valuable challenges the received view that increasing knowledge is the central epistemic value, to be cultivated to the exclusion of any other.

This excessive love of knowledge has been named epistemophilia. [13] The claim is not that love of knowledge is always bad, but that taken to excess, it can and has limited the understanding of epistemic practices and values, because increasing knowledge is not always good, and not the only epistemic good. Epistemophilia perhaps forms the opposite pole to what Alvin Goldman calls "veriphobia" a "deep skepticism or utter repudiation of truth as a viable criterion for studying epistemic phemomena." [14] This excessive enthusiasm for knowledge can lead to claims that knowledge should be maximized, or more plausibly optimized, by responsible epistemic agents, that veritism is the sole standard for epistemic practice, or that knowledge or knowledge conduciveness is the exclusive standard for epistemic good. These claims cannot be sustained.

Epistemophilia shows up in diverse ways. It can take a benign form. Like sinophilia, an enthusiasm for things Chinese, epistemophilia can be an appreciation of and attraction to knowledge that doesn't distort the understanding of its object. But because the study of knowledge is an evaluative and selective enterprise, an excessive and exclusive valuation of knowledge tends to obscure other considerations, so that values other than increasing knowledge are treated as externalities that do not feature in the accounting. Social, political, or ethical concerns are beyond the scope of a self-contained epistemology, and are resisted as alien, and potentially distortive. Epistemophilia yields few resources to analyze epistemic injustice, instead aligning with a view of knowledge as facts observable by anyone, propositions available for anyone's collection, with authority and credit properly accruing to those who acquire knowledge. With such a conception of knowledge, it is easy to see how "patterns of incredulity" are omitted from the field of epistemic concern.[15]

Epistemophilia tends to take all ignorance to be remediable, and best remedied, so the proper response to ignorance is to replace it with knowledge. This attitude conflates all ignorance with simple ignorance, and hence overlooks the ways that the incentives and interests of invested ignorance support a resistance to know or notice certain things. An epistemophilic outlook will also tend to take knowing to be a benign activity, so those adhering to that view will tend not to see the downsides of knowledge increase, such as the appropriation of others' understandings (say in cases of bioprospecting) or the arrogance of an assumed right to take up others' perspectives. Epistemophilia limits the scope of legitimate epistemic interactions to those that in one way or another add to knowledge, and the achievement of knowledge increase is epistemically self justifying. Lorraine Code's descriptive phrase "epistemologies of mastery" captures much of the character of epistemophilic epistemology. An epistemology which takes ignorance seriously is a useful remedy to the problems of epistemophilia.

I adopt the framework of virtue epistemology for my discussion of epistemic agents and their communal practices. Epistemologists in general define and distinguish relevant concepts, identify and defend standards, and explain what we are (and should be) doing, individually and collectively insofar as we are epistemic agents. Epistemology most broadly explains what knowers do and what we need to do in order to qualify as successful knowers. Virtue epistemologies base their analyses on the qualities and dispositions of knowers and tend to offer a less general, less abstracted approach to epistemology, emphasizing applications to persons who know, and persons who engage with others on knowledge-related matters. Thus, for example, epistemology might tell us directly, or indirectly, what experts and discoverers do when they acquire knowledge on behalf of a community.

The position defended here is stronger than the claim that truth-conduciveness is not sufficient for epistemic virtue. Some reliabilist and responsibilist accounts are compatible with that claim, and seek to show what more is needed for an agent to be properly virtuous.[16] It seems counterintuitive to many that conduciveness to truth or knowledge is not *necessary* for epistemic virtue, but I defend this position. The claim is not that an epistemic agent should in general be motivated to seek falsehood, nor that there would be no problems if practicing certain epistemic virtues led to error vastly more often than not. But getting more truth is not the only issue. I will argue that standards for doing well as an epistemic agent are not reducible to the goals of truth and avoidance of error and that we can't tell if a trait is an epistemic virtue by asking whether or not it is maximally or optimally truth-conducive.

My arguments lead to epistemic pluralism in at least two ways: first, I recognize a plurality of values in epistemology. These values are irreducibly plural and do not form a hierarchy—the values of discretion, respect, and credence are not trumped by nor instrumentally justified by reference to veritism or knowledge conduciveness. In many instances knowledge is the important value, but this is not necessarily the case. The second kind of pluralism is pluralism in relation to what is known. The contents of many knowledge systems may converge and overlap significantly, but incommensurate or incompatible pieces can remain. Here, pluralism means a lack of confidence that these ultimately will form a single unified whole, that they can be matched up and so long as they don't match up, at least one party is in error. This is a moderate relativism,[17] which arises because rejecting the view of epistemic agents as knowledge collectors leads to increased emphasis on situational factors.

In contrast to this latter pluralism, consider Peirce's pragmatist theory of truth: "the opinion which is fated to be ultimately agreed to by all who investigate is what we mean by truth, and the object represented is the real."[18] The practices in which such truth can be approximated or attained require dialogue and social cooperation. Hence, such truth requires attention to the community in which the aspiration for agreement is undertaken. I agree with Peirce that the epistemic community is of fundamental importance. He says further that "We individually cannot reasonably hope to attain the ultimate philosophy which we pursue; we can only seek it, therefore, for the *community* of philosophers."[19] But such consensus and unity is problematic for communities, and even for an individual. María Lugones, for example, describes her experience (as Hispanic and lesbian living in the USA) that "some intentions can only be formed and acted on in one, but not in both, cultures, and some intentions can be formed in both but cannot fully inform our actions in both communities. . . . So, my actions may have different understandings in each community."[20] Where this is the case, an aspiration to an understanding that all can share seems problematic—it would mean some significant loss, rather than a gain of coherence. Lugones argues that such risks are real even within one individual: "Because the selves can connect, each can critique the other and avoid the de-moralization of self-betrayal (for example by becoming assimilated to heterosexualism or becoming ignorant of slowly becoming culturally obsolete.)"[21] So the prospect of convergence on exactly one opinion shared by all who investigate is perhaps less likely and more costly than Peirce believed, in some areas at least.

Peirce's work is valuable (as are the ways it has been developed), especially through in its insistence on keeping the path of inquiry open and on the collective nature of the enterprise of inquiry. While I don't engage directly with much of this work, Peirce is a philosophical ancestor I acknowledge, because of his influence on many philosophers I discuss. Arguably Peirce's pragmatic approach entails a capacity to reflect on social conditions and participation as part of responsible epistemic agency. Various contemporary thinkers have included such a capacity as part of intellectual virtue, or epistemic responsibility, emphasizing the need for individuals, groups, and institutions to cultivate such constructive critique. I look, for example, at Jane Braaten's feminist intellectual virtues, Kristina Rolin's requirement for norms of civility in science, and Kathryn Addelson's analysis of professional responsibility.

As these three thinkers make clear, a variety of real world activities mirror some of the implicit or explicit claims about the goals of epistemic agents, and about what counts as knowledge or responsible pursuit of knowledge, made within epistemology. For example, the idea that increasing human knowledge is a good thing occurs in both scientific enterprises (and their funding arrangements) and in various discussions of epistemological theory. An epistemology with room for ignorance, and which recognizes the dangers of epistemophilia, can help us to understand what can go wrong with certain kinds of real world epistemic practice, such as bio-prospecting, appropriation, and exclusion. Criticisms directed at these and other colonialist projects have been generated by (and sometimes at) feminists, and by subaltern theorists. My investigation of such practices derives from epistemic considerations, rather than from a prior political commitment. This approach provides an alternative route to certain conclusions about the requirements of social justice, thus reinforcing the claims feminists and others have made. More precisely, my argument inverts the more common argument that social injustices can have detrimental epistemic consequences. Here, an epistemological error can have detrimental ethical and political consequences.

One advantage of this inversion can be seen in an argument that emerges for greater diversity in knowledge making enterprises, such as scientific research. On a standard argument, epistemic reasons for greater diversity would focus on potential increases in information from diverse sources of critique. But this argument hinges on there being sufficient information gains to off-set any loss of productivity that might result from recalcitrant opposition to diversity and the ways this could inhibit both the new contributions and the divergence of efforts from cooperation (with the old familiar team) to hostility (to new "different" members). My guess is that there could be at least some cases, for some, perhaps lengthy, periods of time, in which the gains do not outweigh the costs. Nevertheless, diversity and inclusion can be defended on epistemic grounds: an epistemic community in which systemic patterns of exclusion of members of some groups from certain roles are minimized is a better epistemic community than one in which such patterns are intractable, in ways that are not reducible to knowledge productivity. The capacity and opportunity to participate in a wide range of epistemic roles is good in itself, good for epistemic agents, independent of how much it contributes to knowledge, and good for epistemic reasons as I will argue later in more detail. Conceivably, the same proportion of truths, even the same truths, could be obtained by collectives with the same memberships, but different arrangements of contributions, roles, and members. Collectives that permit members to cultivate a wide range of epistemic and cognitive skills and virtues are better than those that encourage exclusive narrow specializations or restrict cognitive contributions. Collectives where the opportunities to practice various epistemic roles and cultivate various epistemic virtues are not restricted to narrow and exclusive social groups can hence manifest more epistemic virtue than those with more rigid divisions of labor, and this is so even if there is some loss of productivity or efficiency in the total of true justified beliefs.[22] In other words, the virtue of an epistemic collective or community involves more than its knowledge productivity or efficiency.

Epistemologists have tended to devalue ignorance, but have mostly just neglected it. Unlike evil in ethics (also viewed negatively, to be reduced or avoided) ignorance in epistemology is hardly mentioned. One of the main reasons for the neglect of ignorance is that epistemologists have developed models and accounts of knowledge that *obscure* the role of ignorance. If knowledge is presumed to be a single and unitary kind of thing, the highest and best level of cognitive achievement, then it is the task of epistemologists to offer a characterization of this refined or exalted epistemic state. If ignorance is simply the lack or absence of knowledge, and the epistemological project is to give a proper account of knowledge (its necessary and sufficient conditions), then whatever fails to conform to this account (ignorance) is not salient. If knowledge is a unity, and everyone can know the same things, as stated explicitly in Peirce's description of convergence, and I think presumed elsewhere, then knowers *qua* knowers are interchangeable, and only shallowly interdependent, since in principle anyone can reach the same conclusion. Taking ignorance seriously complicates this picture, but does not eliminate local sharing and convergence of knowledge.

There is perhaps a sense in which ignorance is indirectly valued in science, as it can be seen as an advantage of a theory that it opens up new avenues of research. For example, quantum theory pointed to a great deal of new territory that previously was not known to be unknown. But in such cases, the prospect of knowledge and the opportunity to eliminate ignorance is valued, so it is not really a case where ignorance ought not to be eliminated. John Rawls' famous conception of a "veil of ignorance"[23] may also appear to imply a positive attitude to ignorance, at least as a methodological device. But since this is a pretended ignorance, a positive valuation of genuine ignorance cannot be located here.

In spite of the familiar saying "ignorance is bliss," there is an overwhelming presumption throughout philosophy that ignorance is at best a necessary evil. In ethics, for example, it is usually supposed that ignorance impedes the good judgment necessary for responsible moral agency. Ignorance is often described as lack of knowledge, but it is not a neutral word, and it carries negative connotations, characterizing the one so described as inferior in some way. "Ignorant" describes behavior that is impolite or inappropriate as well as cases when knowledge is lacking or absent. A person exhibiting bad manners is called "ignorant," but the simple implication that she *does not* know better does not always follow, rather it may be implied that she *should* know better, or knows and should behave better. (This is part of the third form of ignorance outlined above, where ignorance refers to a condition of a person or group.) This use of "ignorance" as a term of criticism mirrors a tendency to assume that knowledge is always positive, that all things being equal, more information is better, and, for example, that experts who know better are thereby better judges of what should be done. But when we consider how ignorance and knowledge operate together, it turns out that knowledge and ignorance are not always respectively good and bad.

These negative connotations mean that describing ignorance as valuable will sound odd. But the oddness helps to recall that knowledge has been over-valued, and highlights the need to overcome entrenched assumptions. I retain the term ignorance in spite of its negative connotations in part to emphasize the revisionary nature of the account I offer. In addition, it is quite clear that if ignorance in its own right has valuable epistemic roles, these will not be reducible to instrumental contributions to knowledge increases.

That ignorance has no positive value is not the only assumption taken for granted, rather than explicitly defended by most epistemologists, including virtue epistemologists. Linda Zagzebski's remarks below illustrate the way it appears obvious that increasing knowledge, or truth-conduciveness, is the central epistemic good. Zagzebski sees truth as the goal for epistemic agents, and explicitly commits herself to the truth-conduciveness of intellectual virtues when she writes: "So if it turned out that we were wrong about the truth-conduciveness of one of these traits, that trait would cease to be considered an intellectual virtue. What we would not do is continue to treat it as an intellectual virtue and then go on to declare that intellectual virtues are not necessarily truth-conducive."[24]

Truth-conduciveness, then, is the good, to which epistemic virtues aim, and what enhances truth-conduciveness is instrumentally good. Knowledge and what leads to knowledge together exhaust the domain of epistemic value—only these things are epistemically good. Conversely, ignorance is always bad, to be overcome, reduced, or eliminated. But taking the epistemic community seriously leads to a different picture of epistemic values, a picture in which ignorance has a positive role. Consider the characteristics that are desirable for an epistemic player to possess. Standard virtue-based accounts focus on the acquisition of information through empirical evidence: scrupulousness, rigor, and objectivity are commonly identified as epistemic virtues. Zagzebski's account of such virtues includes "intellectual carefulness, perseverance, humility, vigor, flexibility, courage, and thoroughness, as well as open-mindedness, fair-mindedness, insightfulness, and the virtues opposed to wishful thinking, obtuseness and conformity."[25] A properly community-based epistemology must attend to relationships between knowers characterized by trust, respect, and credibility. Hence the traditional list is incomplete, and must be supplemented with virtues conducive to empathy, cooperation, deference, discrimination, and discretion. I will show that these features of epistemic interactions at times require the tolerance and even promotion of ignorance. For example, when persons must be selective about what to reveal and share, in exercising the virtue of discretion, they are concerned with ignorance as much as with knowledge. A number of epistemologies are flawed by a failure to recognize virtues such as discretion, but understanding the role of ignorance is essential for understanding many epistemic interactions. This means that an epistemic agent's ignorance ought not to be presumed to be vice or failure, and an agent's knowledge need not be taken as equivalent to success. Epistemological accounts that overlook or deny the importance of ignorance will not account for the virtues involved in interactions between knowers. Part of being a knower in community is understanding the norms of nondisclosure and noninvestigation, and these, I argue, value forms of ignorance. An epistemic agent should not always seek to remedy her own states of ignorance, nor should she set out to communicate all she knows to others. Negative and positive epistemic value do not map on to the ignorance and knowledge that knowers need to navigate in practice.

Ignorance is indispensable, at a theoretical level, most obviously for an account of epistemic interdependence. Reliance on others for knowledge is an ineliminable part of epistemic life, which is one of the most important reasons for taking a nonindividualistic approach to the theory of knowledge. The division of epistemic labor involves ignorance, as others know what I do not, so understanding ignorance sheds further light on socially instituted roles for experts and other epistemic authorities. A simple conception of the value of knowledge yields a misleadingly simple justification of epistemic authority. Those who are experts are closer to, or have a more extended view of, an information domain that would look the same to anyone with the opportunity to make the same observations. On such a view, epistemic authority is unproblematic, because anyone, in principle, could have it. When I encounter others who know what I do not, they are entitled (if not obliged) to share information with me, and I am entitled to acquire knowledge on their say so (there is more to say about conditions for testimonial transmission, but here, I am more concerned with the structure than details). Those who are experts happen to know more than others do, and the knowledge that counts is that which is authorized by the proper institutions. Institutions and practices that successfully produce knowledge are thereby justified; firstly, because knowledge is considered to be a good thing in its own right, so producing it is good, and secondly, because since knowledge is actually produced, it seems that there cannot be too much wrong with the practices that generate it. These practices must be sufficiently neutral and nondistortive to produce knowledge. Additionally, knowledge is thought to be a good for everyone, as the phrase "for the human community" suggests. In practice, knowledge benefits are far from universal. For example, medical research is said to be for the good of humanity. But in fact the benefits tend to go to research corporations, and to patients from the wealthier sections of wealthier communities, whereas participants in medical trials often come from vastly different communities and social groups, generally those who are much less advantaged. The benefits and costs are not evenly distributed, and references to "human community" tend to obscure these patterns.

But the lack of attention to the exact meaning of "human knowledge" or "humanity's knowledge" also obscures whether information is widely known or highly restricted, specialized but accessible, buried in neglected books or data-bases, part of a small group's "secret business" and so on. In other words, "human knowledge" depends on complex interdependence between people, institutions, and communities, past and present. Thus epistemology requires a social dimension.

The book's main aim is to set up a general argument that works on epistemological terms and that can be applied in various types of cases. My discussions tend to use abstract examples, for two reasons. First, I start from existing discussions in epistemology, so inherit that level of abstraction, and second, abstraction enables arguments to be presented more cleanly and efficiently. However, those benefits are counterweighted by the danger of omitting or eliding "details" that would make an important difference to the arguments. The example in chapter 1 of Dennis and Christopher is an example of how something that looks plausible in the abstract (the claim that epistemic independence is superior to dependence) looks less plausible in a variety of concrete versions. While my own examples tend towards abstraction, I hope they are both rich enough to achieve real-world plausibility, and general enough to suggest their wider applications.

In chapter 1, I develop an account of epistemic community, taking interdependence as fundamental. I show that even when an account starts with an ideal of knowledge collecting, as soon as cooperation is admitted as part of epistemic practice, knowledge maximizing (or optimizing) has to be supplemented with virtues of cooperation. An epistemic theory might also offer ways to evaluate the community as a whole: Is the community sustainable, are its actual practices those its members would thoughtfully endorse? Is the community virtuous? Relying on knowledge as the sole evaluative standard yields unsatisfactory answers to such questions.

In chapter 2, I focus on interdependence in the forms of trust and reliance. Trust is a source of knowledge that cannot be reduced to treating persons and their claims as evidence and it involves ignorance. Thus, the reevaluation of ignorance emerges from the starting point of epistemic community. In chapter 3 I argue further that the epistemic responsibilities of expert knowers are not limited to the provision or acquisition of accurate information. I show that an approach to knowledge that incorporates ignorance and starts from the ways that virtuous knowers engage with one another is a promising way to analyze practical epistemic concerns.

In chapter 4, I make explicit an argument for epistemic pluralism. I consider the roles of ignorance in knowledge transactions between social groups: especially knowing about other groups and acquiring knowledge from other groups. I show how this revised epistemology differs from and contributes to issues in feminist epistemology. I discuss feminists who recognize that epistemic practices reflect patterns of subordination and oppression between social groups and have shown how exclusionary and hierarchical patterns of interdependence within and between social groups affect trust, credibility, and authority. While I tend to agree with feminist diagnoses of ethical and political dimensions to epistemic practices (and my account is strongly influenced by feminist critiques of epistemic individualism[26]), my arguments start from an account of epistemic dependence within epistemology, and extend toward political considerations, rather than applying feminist concerns to theories and practices concerning knowledge.[27] Hence there are differences as well as convergences between my project and others in feminist epistemology. First, ignorance usually appears in feminist discussions as a problem to be identified and overcome. Problematic forms of ignorance include an ignorance that is complicit in privilege (invested ignorance), and ignorance that keeps members of some group from full participation in epistemic practices (exclusionary ignorance). (These need not be exclusive categories.) My aim is not to deny that ignorance can be involved in oppression, but to show that there are other possibilities: just as knowledge is not always good, ignorance is not always bad. Second, my project is initially motivated not by an understanding of and opposition to gender oppression, but by an explanation and revaluation of ignorance within epistemology. The arguments developed here show that epistemology on its own terms needs to take seriously its common ground with considerations that have been raised by feminists whether or not an explicitly feminist agenda is adopted. Locating my project within feminist epistemology shows how it contributes to social epistemology more broadly, as the relevant parts[28] of feminist epistemology fall broadly into that category.

The project as a whole demonstrates that taking account of ignorance in epistemological theory enhances an adequate analysis of a range of epistemic practices that cannot be reduced to knowledge maximizing. Ignorance is both theoretically indispensable to epistemological analyses and practically invaluable for a community of knowers. According to many accounts of epistemic value, failure to remedy a lack or absence of knowledge that could be remedied would be bad: if cases of ignorance are unavoidable, they are regrettable, and a virtuous or responsible or ideal epistemic agent would seek to minimize them. On this common understanding of knowledge and its value, reasons to forgo the acquisition and sharing of knowledge would have to come from outside epistemology—from convention, taboo, politeness, moral restraint, respect for privacy, and/or all kinds of pragmatic reasons. But there are *epistemic* reasons for knowers to maintain rather than remedy ignorance, in both the first person case, and with respect to other epistemic agents, in cooperative cases. Just as it is a mistake to take knowledge to be always good, rejecting ignorance as always negative is too hasty.

NOTES

1. Even if ignorance is not considered valuable, this is a striking omission, not paralleled in other philosophical contexts. For example, virtue is often explained relative to vice, understanding justice is aided by understanding forms of injustice, such as oppression and exploitation, and teaching critical thinking typically includes sections on fallacious reasoning.

2. Brian Yazzie Burkhart makes a similar point in comparing the traditional Western approach to epistemology with American Indian epistemology and metaphysics: "From the perspective of Western Philosophy, it is generally thought that more knowledge is always better." Brian Y. Burkhart, "What Coyote and Thales Can Teach Us," in *American Indian Thought*, ed. Anne Waters (Oxford: Blackwell Publishing, 2004), 18.

3. Compare the discussion of epistemic value pluralism in Guy Axtell, "Expanding Epistemology: A Responsibilist Approach," *Philosophical Papers* 37, no. 1 (2008): 51–87.

4. . For survey of work in revisionary epistemology, see Axtell, "Expanding Epistemology," 51–87.

5. Alvin Goldman's social epistemics is exemplary in this respect. I later take issue with his emphasis on veritism, but not with his overall motivation.

6. Charles Mills, *The Racial Contract* (Ithaca, NY: Cornell University Press, 1997).

7. Miranda Fricker, *Epistemic Injustice: Power and the Ethics of Knowing* (Oxford: Oxford University Press, 2007). See also Miranda Fricker, "Powerlessness and Social Interpretation," *Episteme: A Journal of Social Epistemology* 3, no. 1–2 (2006): 96–108.

8. See, for example, Jason Dana and George Loewenstein, "A Social Science Perspective on Gifts to Physicians from Industry," *Journal of the American Medical Association* 290, no. 2 (2003): 252–55.

9. Lorraine Code distinguishes an "ignorant ignorance" from a "conscious, self-congratulatory ignorance." Lorraine Code, "The Power of Ignorance," in *Race and Epistemologies of Ignorance*, ed. Shannon Sullivan and Nancy Tuana (Albany: State University of New York Press, 2007), 215.

10. Sandra Harding, "Two Influential Theories of Ignorance and Philosophy's Interests in Ignoring Them," *Hypatia* 21, no. 3 (2006): 20–36.

11. Nancy D. Campbell, "Reconstructing Science and Technology Studies: Views from Feminist Standpoint Theory," *Frontiers: A Journal of Women Studies* 30, no. 1 (2009): 1–29.

12. For example, see Alison Bailey, "Strategic Ignorance," in *Race and Epistemologies of Ignorance*, ed. Shannon Sullivan and Nancy Tuana (Albany: State University of New York Press, 2007), 77–94; and papers in *Frontiers: A Journal of Women Studies (Special Issue) Knowledge that Matters: Feminist Epistemology, Methodology and Science Studies* 30, no. 1 (2009).

13. The term "epistemophilia" is Lorraine Code's.

14. Alvin Goldman, *Knowledge in a Social World* (Oxford: Clarendon Press, 1999), 7.

15. The phrase "patterns of incredulity" is taken from Lorraine Code, *Ecological Thinking* (Oxford: Oxford University Press, 2006), see especially 163–200.

16. See, for example, G. Axtell, "Recent Work on Virtue Epistemology," *American Philosophical Quarterly* 34, no. 1 (1997): 1–26, and Axtell, "Expanding Epistemology," 51–87.

17. For a discussion of how such relativism works, see Lorraine Code, *Rhetorical Spaces: Essays on Gendered Locations* (New York: Routledge, 1995), especially 185–207.

18. C. S. Peirce, "How to Make Our Ideas Clear," in *Charles S. Peirce: Selected Writings*, ed. Philip Wiener (New York: Dover Publications, 1958), 133.

19. C. S. Peirce, "Some Consequences of Four Incapacities," in *Charles S. Peirce: Selected Writings*, ed. Philip Wiener (New York, Dover Publications, 1958), 40.

20. Maria Lugones, "Hispaneando y Lesbiando: On Sarah Hoagland's *Lesbian Ethics,*" *Hypatia* 5, no. 3 (1990): 144.

21. Lugones, "Hispaneando y Lesbiando," 144.

22. These are notoriously difficult to count. Note also that the development of knowledge is not eliminated as an important epistemic value, but it is not a trumping value, and sometimes can be balanced against others.

23. John Rawls, *A Theory of Justice* (London: Oxford University Press, 1973).

24. Linda Zagzebski, *Virtues of the Mind* (Cambridge: Cambridge University Press, 1996), 185.

25. Zagzebski, *Virtues of the Mind*, 155.

26. While the tradition of epistemic individualism remains strong, work by feminist epistemologists and social epistemologists has made epistemic communities and epistemic dependence (for example testimony) much more central and mainstream topics within epistemology. Heidi E. Grasswick and Mark Owen Webb point out: "The field is burgeoning; a search of the *Philosopher's Index* reveals that although nothing was published before 1981 that was categorized as both feminist and epistemology, soon after, the rate of publication in feminist epistemology rose to between 15 and 25 articles per year." H. Grasswick and M. O. Webb, "Feminist epistemology as social epistemology," *Social Epistemology* 16, no. 3 (2002), 185.

27. Admittedly, this generalization exaggerates the difference between my approach and of others in feminist epistemology, and does not do justice to the diversity of approaches that attract the label "feminist epistemology" nor to the influence of feminist philosophy on my work. Nevertheless, I think the arguments about ignorance and epistemic dependence developed here could be accepted by someone who does not initially recognize the need to consider gender and other social group differences in order to understand knowledge practices.

28. Here, I am concerned with feminist epistemology that explores the patterns of credence, authority and acknowledgment that align with stereotypes and subordination-domination relations, rather than those branches of feminist epistemology concerned with women's ways of knowing and the like. The point is not that these can't intersect and overlap, but rather to indicate the broad area closest to my own concerns.

Chapter One

Epistemic Dependence: Beyond Facts

> Now, what I want is, Facts. Teach these boys and girls nothing but Facts. Facts alone are wanted in life. Plant nothing else, and root out everything else. You can only form the minds of reasoning animals upon Facts: nothing else will ever be of any service to them.[1]

As recent work has established testimony as a legitimate source of knowledge, epistemic dependence has become an important topic within epistemology. Edward Craig, for example, develops an account of knowledge based on inquirers and informants.[2] I am not concerned with a particular analysis of testimony, but will take for granted that knowledge can be transferred between agents. I aim to show both that agents acquire facts from one another in at least two distinct ways and that epistemic agents depend on one another for more than testimonial information. Standard treatments of epistemic dependence overlook these features, due to two pervasive errors. First, it is commonly assumed that epistemic dependence is inferior to independent knowledge acquisition. By closely examining an instance of this comparison in the first part of this chapter, I show that there is no general way to judge dependence and independence against each other as their value and appropriateness vary with context. Second, it is assumed that the scope of epistemic dependence is limited to testimonial interaction, or transmission of facts. I argue for a richer notion of epistemic dependence than is generally found in epistemological discussions by looking more widely at what an epistemic community provides for its members. This argument begins in the second part of this chapter, with a characterization of the central epistemic duty as the duty to seek more evidence. I show that this account invokes epistemic community with insufficient detail and complexity, even for its own stated purposes. In contrast, I explore an alternative account which takes a broader view of the values and practices of an epistemic community. The importance and indispensability of ignorance emerge from this richer and more clearly articulated account of epistemic dependence.

TESTIMONY: KNOWING AND TELLING

Philosophers interested in knowledge have tended to concentrate on the generation of precise definitions of knowledge and related concepts and on the refutation of skeptical challenges.[3] Within analytic philosophy, less attention has been paid directly to analyzing and evaluating the characteristics and practices of epistemic agents, especially those characteristics and practices involved in epistemic dependence. Thus, even within recent work on testimony and social epistemology, there has been insufficient acknowledgement of the importance of epistemic community. Even within virtue epistemology, when virtues (qualities of knowers) provide the framework for epistemological discussion, much of the literature still exhibits what Lorraine Code has called the "autonomy obsession."[4] This phrase refers to the concentration of theoretical attention on individualistic features of epistemic practice while communal practices are barely acknowledged, or taken simply to be reducible to collections of individualistic activities.

Most broadly, an epistemic community is a network of relationships between agents engaged in epistemic activities and practices. Paradigmatic epistemic practices involve acquisition, distribution and sharing of knowledge, including investigation, education, archiving, informing, learning and reflecting upon these activities. The term "epistemic community" is analogous to "scientific community," which has a range of uses. It sometimes means scientific practitioners in general, sometimes those pursuing a specific project, and sometimes the whole group served by the labor of experts in a variety of disciplines producing a particular set of knowledge bases. Similarly, with respect to an epistemic community, we might talk of a particular domain of interactions or transactions, consider the division of epistemic labor between experts and "folk" or invoke the community as the background to and context for all these practices. In all of these enterprises, while testimonial exchange is significant, epistemic agents also judge credibility, establish justification, critically examine standards, revise practices, endorse or challenge each others' habits and practices and so on. The claim that to be a knower is to be a knower in community is not novel, but the implications of this claim for understanding epistemic values merit further exploration.

I will argue that full membership of an epistemic community includes having the connections to other agents that enable (but also sometimes restrict) my epistemic agency. The community of which I am a member is the initial environment that nurtures and develops and then maintains my capacities. It provides references for norms and standards, and the context for acknowledgement and credit. A mature epistemic agent has the competence to engage with other agents and can recognize and be recognized by them as an epistemic agent. As well as exchanging information, she can give and receive criticism and expand or constrain the scope of discussion. In particular contexts, such as an institution, a research group, or a classroom, community membership may be understood more narrowly, to refer to engagement with particular others, an enculturation into particular, perhaps discipline—or institution-based knowledge practices. In some instances, for example learning a (first or subsequent) language, reliance on authority is paramount, but in other cases such as some consciousness raising groups, one's own experience is the basis for learning.[5] In both cases, though, there is a communal context, in which understandings, competences, and justifications are developed.

Many references to epistemic community (sometimes made via an unexamined idea of human knowledge) manifest an excessive, usually exclusive focus on the value of knowledge-conduciveness. When increasing knowledge is seen as the central and perhaps the only epistemic value for a community, too little attention is paid to other features that, among other things, form a necessary background to transmission and disclosure. By taking the epistemic community seriously, I will show not only that knowledge increase does not exhaust the domain of epistemic value, but that the broader range of epistemic values include positive roles for ignorance.

Although testimony is the most widely examined form of epistemic dependence, testimony and its value both tend to be understood narrowly. Often the acquisition of information from others via testimony is the only consideration of epistemic dependence, perhaps because dependence on testimony is ubiquitous. Countless examples can be collected from theoretical and practical domains to show that knowledge gained from others constitutes a significant proportion (perhaps most) of what we take ourselves to know. We depend on others for corroboration as well as for otherwise inaccessible information. My first response to a surprising or interesting observation is to ask my companion "did you see that?" I check my interpretation of an event in narrating it (or I test and develop my philosophical analysis of some problem by exposing it to peer review) so others confirm or amend the understandings that emerge from observations and inferences. The contributions that others make to my knowledge both as sources and as reinforcement cannot be replaced by autonomous efforts. But epistemic dependence extends beyond testimony.

It is taken for granted by some authors that there is something second rate about knowledge acquired through testimony, but this assumption is mistaken. The assumptions that knowledge increase provides the only standard for evaluating epistemic practice, and that autonomy is superior to dependence, detract from current epistemologies both by excluding some practices from consideration and by undervaluing dependency when interactions are considered. To some philosophers, while they admit that knowledge can be acquired through testimony, it seems obvious that a recipient of knowledge is inferior in some sense to the original source. This denigration of epistemic dependence is reasonably common, but it constitutes a significant obstacle to the development of an adequate theoretical account of epistemic community.

Consider the following two examples of philosophers (both epistemic virtue theorists) claiming that knowing by being told is inferior to knowing by investigation.

Jonathan Kvanvig asks us to:

> suppose there are two cognitive beings, S1 and S2, each of whom knows all and only what the other one knows. They acquire their knowledge in different ways, however, S1 knows on the basis of investigation; S2 knows on the basis of being told by S1. In such a case, S1 is a superior cognitive being to S2. However, this superiority cannot be explained in terms of the knowledge or justification which attaches to each.[6]

Linda Zagzebski concludes that epistemic independence is superior to dependence from a similar comparison:

> Taliaferro compares two omniscient beings he calls Dennis and Christopher. Both Dennis and Christopher believe all and only true propositions, but Dennis believes them because he has learned them from Christopher, who we will suppose has "seen" the truths for himself or has learned them by his own power. . . . But Taliaferro points out that Dennis is cognitively inferior to Christopher because of the way in which he gets his knowledge. We might say that in this case what Dennis is like and what he does is only accidentally connected to his acquiring the truth, and his cognitive worth is the worth of the perfect computer.[7]

Both Kvanvig and Zagzebski (like Taliaferro) take it as obvious and uncontroversial that the discoverer is in some important way a better epistemic agent than the trustor. As Zagzebski puts it, "intuitively Christopher is superior in knowledge to Dennis because he possesses greater cognitive power. But since he does not know more true propositions than Dennis does, his superiority in knowledge must involve superior quality."[8]

Zagzebski and Kvanvig take it as axiomatic that dependence on others is inferior to independent investigation, and that trusting an authority has little or no cognitive standing. But this picture of epistemic dependence is misleading, with respect to both the responsibility of an epistemic authority and the activity of an epistemic dependant. It is flawed precisely because it fails to take account of the full range of virtues exercised by epistemic agents even when we construe them as responsible hearers and deliverers of testimony.

Zagzebski's account can be taken as a case study in the "autonomy obsession"[9] that grounds the judgment that dependent knowers are inferior. Misconceptions about autonomy lead to the overvaluation of independent investigation. It is worth examining this position in some detail, because its intuitive appeal is strong, although the assumption it represents is false and distorting.

Zagzebski likens Dennis to a "perfect computer." Although computers[10] can perform many complex tasks faster than human agents, there is a sense in which humans possess greater cognitive power than computing machines. Computers depend on human initiative. Zagzebski's remark presumably indicates that Dennis lacks initiative or autonomy. He is a passive recipient of information from Christopher, who enters the data, so to speak.

But there is another way to assess Dennis' cognitive value. While we *could* see Dennis as a computer that Christopher is filling with data, we could equally see *Christopher*, the perfect oracle, *as being used* by Dennis as an *instrument* for knowledge. Perhaps Christopher has no cognitive dispositions other than to investigate and disclose as directed. Dennis could be Christopher's resource for storing information, even for performing calculations on data, but Christopher could be Dennis' field worker who gathers information for a complex project. (Perhaps either one could be thought of as part of the other's extended mind.) Since the metaphor of an epistemic instrument could apply to either party, it tells us nothing whatsoever about the relative "cognitive worth" of Dennis and Christopher, and their respective practices.[11] Given that both parties can be described as a mere epistemic instrument and each characterized as a responsible agent of inquiry, it is not clear that a recipient of information is passive,[12] nor that an investigator operates independently.

Zagzebski takes it that Dennis must have no more resources than a computer to judge and assess the information coming to him from Christopher, but it is not clear how she would defend this and especially unclear that parties to ordinary epistemic interactions could be so characterized. My acceptance of information from an authority may be critical or uncritical, but so can my own investigation. Just as I may be culpably gullible when I accept a deal proposed by an insurance agent making an unsolicited phone call, I may investigate uncritically—I go to the library all by myself, but read only the books I happen to see on the shelf, neither undertaking a catalogue search nor consulting the competent research librarian available to me. I could be in the library to pursue my own research agenda, or fulfilling a task someone else assigned to me. Zagzebski does not distinguish the initiation of the task (which could be self- or other-directed) from the approach to the task which can be undertaken more or less responsibly. The example does not show that greater cognitive worth can be attributed to either a self- or other-directed activity.

Zagzebski tells us that "what Dennis is like and what he does is only accidentally connected to his acquiring the truth," but this claim has little plausibility with respect to actual epistemic agents involved in collaborative ventures and seems odd, even with respect to her own conceived case. Admittedly, Dennis is not displaying any cognitive characteristics other than a disposition to accept what he is told. We have no information about any of the circumstances under which Dennis obtains information from Christopher. But we do know that this dependence on Christopher's authority is a truth-conducive disposition, and it would seem unlikely that Dennis has acquired such a good informant by accident.

Even if Dennis had encountered Christopher by accident, this would not show that his continued reliance fails to be responsible.[13] If he comes to recognize the quality of his informant (*ex hypothesis* perfectly reliable) and nothing suggests that his belief would be unjustified (there are no defeaters) then his credence is well-grounded.[14] Imagine that I enroll in a college chosen at random (or at least without any careful and appropriate selection process) in order to major in philosophy. (Perhaps I know that I can transfer if this does not work out.) Purely by luck, I end up an excellent department with great professors, and I complete the degree. While I am studying, the fact that I originally enrolled without good reason does not seem to undermine the warrant of my subsequent assessment of the teachers as reliable, nor does it contaminate the warrant of my acceptance of their authority and guidance. Dennis' continued access to the truth need not be accidental, if it is based on a justified (emergent) recognition of an authority who is perfectly reliable. In fact, since Christopher is an impeccable provider of information, Dennis' source is much better than those on which most of us depend. Since, in this case, Dennis trusts a perfectly reliable authority, there is no reason for his critical faculties to be triggered. (If Christopher were not reliable, then his behavior would be misleading, and likely not virtuous, so the comparison loses its point.)

If Dennis is a responsible believer, then there is no reason to suppose him cognitively inferior to Christopher. If he is not a responsible believer, for example, if he lacks critical faculties, or has a disposition to believe such that his critical faculties would not be triggered in appropriate conditions, then he would be inferior to a responsible and competent epistemic agent. But in that case, the comparison would not tell us anything about these kinds of interaction in general. The example would be question-begging if it were to compare a defective trustor with a competent investigator. Both trust and investigation can be undertaken carefully or carelessly.

Delivering and learning from testimony are both complex, cognitively demanding activities.[15] Once trust and dependence are recognized as requiring virtues of commitment and discrimination, and sharing information is recognized as requiring discretion as well as accurate disclosure, the complex roles of epistemic agents understood as interacting members of epistemic communities begin to emerge. But before outlining these roles, one more aspect of dependence needs to be considered, since there is an important sense in which Dennis' access to information might be seen as accidental or contingent. It depends on another epistemic agent, who might not continue to be a good source.[16] The point is not merely that our knowledge is mediated, as access to knowledge is often mediated by instruments, but that other knowers are unlike thermostats or telescopes. They have human failings as well as being prone to inaccuracy through sensory errors analogous to mechanical breakdown. Perhaps this consideration motivates the intuition that Dennis is inferior. On this interpretation, independent investigation is superior to dependence because knowledge unmediated by other agents is not vulnerable to their fallibility, veniality or unpredictability. It may appear that the warrant for knowledge decreases as we pass along a testimonial chain[17] and therefore, that belief grounded in testimony degenerates epistemically. As David Hume famously suggests, the longer a chain of testimony, the greater the possibility of deliberate deceit or inadvertent error just because more people are involved.

However, just as a knower is capable of misleading the audience in a wider range of ways than is a mere instrument (a human source might deliberately fail to cooperate, but a mechanical instrument cannot do that), another knower offers significant advantages as a source of information. Other epistemic agents can be insightful and responsive in ways that even the best search engines might never approximate. Admittedly, Dennis' access to knowledge depends on Christopher's continued cooperation, and this is not something over which Dennis has any control. But to say that testifiers are not mere *instruments* of knowledge is not to say that they are *deficient* instruments. Agents are different from instruments, and a distinct range of skills and virtues is necessary for engaging with other knowers. The important point is not that a person may be more or less liable to error than an instrument, but that we must understand epistemic dependence on other knowers differently from dependence on instruments. In accounting for epistemic cooperation, we need reference to trust, credibility and integrity—the characteristics of epistemic agents who do more than deliver and receive information like computers. No real knower is an independent investigator like Christopher. We are all, like Dennis, substantially reliant on other epistemic agents who, in many actual cases, reciprocally depend on us. A large part of our cognitive agency involves the construction and maintenance of appropriate epistemic relationships with others in the epistemic community. Dennis is doing particularly well in regard to finding and using good sources of information, such as other knowers to trust. Ordinarily, an epistemic agent might be faulted for unwise reliance on only one source of information, but well-founded confidence in a perfect oracle is an exceptional case. The possibility of being led astray would not, in any case, establish that in general dependence is inferior to investigation, only that there may be better and worse ways of depending on other members of the epistemic community. That my community is not error-free does not show that that relying on it is inferior to independence.

The judgment that investigation is superior to dependence seems to be founded on the priority of autonomy. Dennis' presumed inferiority derives precisely from his apparent failure to display autonomy. But as I have suggested, the judgment that he lacks autonomy is plausible only if autonomy is supposed to rule out *any* dependence, and if epistemic dependence is taken to be passive and uncritical. But my acquisition of knowledge from another can involve agency, discrimination, and critical reflection. As I work on a joint paper about intellectual property, I acquire knowledge from my collaborative partner, who is a lawyer, and she learns from me. Such collaborative projects show that autonomy and dependence are not mutually exclusive, and cooperative practices work precisely because they can be combined.

Zagzebski's position exemplifies problems that arise from excessive emphasis on autonomy and the authority of an individual knower. She upholds the traditional and still common view of independence even as she develops a virtue epistemology that is progressive in other ways. This individualism renders her account of this example erroneous, but also impoverishes her overall position as it becomes very difficult to extend her account of epistemic virtues to include trust, discretion, credence, and authority.

There is something wrong with a theory that requires that the persons on whom we depend for knowledge can be nothing more than sources like other non-agential sources in the epistemic landscape, or that they ought to be evaluated in the same terms of reliability and unreliability as instruments like telescopes.[18] My point here is that instrumentalization and objectification is *epistemically* misguided. Important features of the epistemic landscape are obscured by such attitudes. Persons are not merely sources of knowledge or information like instruments.[19] Their epistemic importance to me is much broader than a role as simple providers of data with disconcertingly variable degrees of reliability. Others are *exemplars* and *mentors* for me as a knower, others enable me to construct, adjust and fine-tune my understandings, others *inspire* (or *curb*) my creativity and can help me to reflect on and improve my epistemic standards and practices. Epistemic virtues include those that encourage other members of the community to do well with knowledge, not just to collect or acquire it, but to engage authoritatively with others, to seek appropriate others on whom to depend, to trust and defer wisely, to consult in order to calibrate one's own standards, to assist others to maintain appropriate standards (directly or indirectly, for example, by cultivating systems that reduce bias or enhance inclusiveness), and so on. We need to be able to defend our claims to know, not just check whether they coincide with other results, so we need interactions with epistemic agents, not just encounters with sources of information, however accurate.

If Christopher were really so cognitively superior, one might suppose that he, in contrast to Dennis, could serve as an exemplar for ordinary epistemic agents. But there are many contexts in which dependence is proper and appropriate, and this is an inappropriate, even empty, model. The strategy of independence not only demands massive expenditure of time and energy, but also would result in an enormous restriction on the information an agent can acquire. Without reliance on others' reports, Christopher would be restricted to what he could learn from his own observations and inferences. Hence the scope of his knowledge would be severely impoverished and there is a great deal he could never know. Perhaps more importantly, the way Christopher treats Dennis is not necessarily the way we would like to be treated by our epistemic comrades in situations of knowledge acquisition. Suppose Christopher were Dennis' teacher. In some contexts it may be virtuous or responsible to treat a student as an empty vessel, to be filled with all the knowledge that the authority has painstakingly acquired.[20] There are particular goals, such as the memorization of a text for an examination or rote learning of multiplication tables, but data entry is far from typical either of education, or of epistemic interaction in general. If I were consulting an expert, such as a medical practitioner or investment advisor, who responded with a Christopher-like disposition to inform me of everything that person knew without any consideration for my epistemic agency, I might be overwhelmed with too much information, and I might fail to acquire any relevant knowledge at all. I might obtain a great deal of useless information, but no help in dealing with it. If my tax advisor recites the manual of tax law, including various appeals and judgments, she is probably not really helping me. Insofar as consultation is a joint endeavor between knowers—however different their competences with respect to the domain—if the expert transmits information in a way that denies the agency of the recipient, he or she not only manifests disrespect to that person, but undermines the whole enterprise of consulting an expert.

With respect to relying on testimony, there is the same kind of default justification as there is with respect to relying on senses and memory. Most of the time, I simply take it for granted that my perceptions are reliable. I only need critical reflection in exceptional cases, so those faculties remain in the background until called into play, when the default justification is over-ridden. Surely, most of the time I take it that people I ask for information (such as a price of an item in a shop) tell me the truth. It takes a lot to undercut the default position, and it *should.*

In general, I am better off to rely on a fallible medical practitioner (I don't know any infallible ones) than I would be to self-diagnose. We are better off with the division of epistemic labor in a community than with a set of infallible instruments to use in solitary pursuits of knowledge. Different contingencies arise with respect to epistemic dependence than with respect to factual investigation, but this does not show that cognitive success in one sphere is superior to success in the other. In fact, successful trustors can almost certainly acquire knowledge on a wider range of topics than can successful solitary investigators.

We can now see that epistemic authority carries with it responsibilities that extend beyond the accurate delivery of information. The point is not that investigators are *never* superior to trustors, but rather that cognitive superiority and epistemic virtue do not track the epistemic roles of investigator and trustor. These roles, and their respective values are more complex and variable than either Zagzebski or Kvanvig recognize, and reliability with respect to content is not sufficient for epistemic virtue in either role. When testimony proceeds well, and knowledge is properly transmitted and acquired, both testifiers and trustors must exercise judgment and discrimination about what is disclosed and believed. Just as excessive credulity should be avoided, so should a rigid insistence on independence and an indiscriminate delivery of all the information. Theorists need to recognize that a knower who knows only on the basis of investigation will not necessarily be superior to one who instances the virtues of responsible dependence and trust.

This is not to imply that every dependent agent is responsible. We can be culpably gullible by, for example, ignoring the possibility that another agent has incentives to deceive, or culpably exploit another's investigations by, for example, plagiarizing. But responsible dependence need not be inferior to independent investigation, and if both are undertaken responsibly, which one turns out to be the better course of action will depend on the context. There is no simple assessment of the respective value of trust and investigation considered in abstraction. The intuition that leads many theorists including Zagzebski and Kvanvig to suppose otherwise is unfounded and unsustainable.

While there is no doubt that it matters how knowledge is acquired, it is a mistake to insist that Christopher, a discoverer, instances a higher standard of epistemic virtue than Dennis, a trustor. First, there is no context-free way to make the comparison, and second, spelling out some plausible contexts of dependence reveals a variety of ways that dependence can be fully responsible and virtuous. Zagzebski is right that the same levels of knowledge in circumstances with varying epistemic practices can be evaluated differently. I disagree with her view of autonomy and dependence, both the hierarchy in which she orders them and the way she characterizes them. But the general point is correct—knowledge quantity is not the only way to judge the epistemic value of a situation or practice.

More importantly, accounts such those presented above by Kvanvig and Zagzebski fail to recognize that when autonomy is exercised in a social or communal context (and receiving testimony will always be social in some sense) it is influenced by the practices and attitudes of other parties. As a teacher, I can work in the classroom in a way that enhances the autonomy of my students, or I can discourage it, precisely in the way that I convey information and encourage my students to acquire new knowledge.[21] For example, I can encourage active participation and questioning from some students while I expect others to stay quiet and receptive.[22]

Autonomy, the value that supposedly makes Christopher superior, is not maximized by the knowers in the situations described by Zagzebski and Kvanvig. Both "superior" knowers in question might be ignoring the autonomy of their fellow knowers by treating them as information sponges. The assumption of investigative superiority obscures the fact that relationships involving epistemic dependence can encourage or undermine autonomy on the side of the recipient of knowledge.

Consider a pediatrician telling a mother about her child's medical condition. The conversation can consist of her being told the best information the specialist can provide, or the discussion can occur as a collaborative exchange in which she can question, even challenge the expert. Then they discuss treatment—either the mother can be told what would be best, or a plan can be jointly worked out. In respect to both the epistemic transaction in which the mother acquires knowledge, and the development of a course of action, her autonomy can be enhanced or undermined. In either case, the information acquired, or the action undertaken may not be at issue. Imagine, also, members of an indigenous group discussing their language with an academic researcher. Their autonomy might be disregarded or enhanced in the transaction, depending on whether they are seen as mere instruments to provide information, as authoritative experts, as people expected to learn and conform to the linguist's conclusions, and on the context of the research project and its wider ramifications.[23]

The distinction between epistemic processes involving mutual recognition or expert pronouncement does not depend simply on how the learner (or mother in the above case) approaches the situation. An expert or testifier may deliver information in such a way that space for the audience to exercise autonomy is diminished. In such cases, we do not consider the *recipient* of such an attitude to be cognitively irresponsible. If I am treated paternalistically by a medical practitioner who tells me about the treatment she considers best, but does not inform me about alternative options, there is an epistemic fault on the side of the practitioner. At least sometimes, those conveying information to others have a capacity and responsibility to consider the agency and autonomy of those who are dependent.[24] A learner can approach another's testimony in more or less gullible or critical ways, and an expert can encourage one or the other attitude. Both can conduct themselves in more or less epistemically responsible ways, but these need not reduce to how much knowledge has been transmitted or acquired.

Standard discussions of epistemic virtues list those which would be useful for a scientist proposing and testing hypotheses. Open-mindedness, intellectual sobriety, and courage are the virtues of an investigator, of a Christopher, not a Dennis, although both, it seems, may be proportioning belief to evidence. For such virtues, perhaps an ideal of truth-conduciveness can work. But according to the standard of truth-conduciveness, Christopher's total disclosure is unproblematic. And contextual considerations such as the type of relationship between Dennis and Christopher or the circumstances of each party are also rendered invisible. As discussed above, a teacher ought not simply impart data, but in contrast acting as the eyes and ears for a person whose mobility is restricted (or investigating as a research assistant might proceed, bracketing her own selective processes and interests) could be an admirable and epistemically valuable contribution.

Epistemic virtue theory has the potential to offer resources for understanding a range of activities and values. Traditional theories of knowledge tend to formulate the conditions for knowledge in ways that make no reference to a person and her character, dispositions or traits, referring exclusively to some variation of "justified true belief" (with some post-Gettier extension).[25] Virtue epistemologists seek to describe enduring and developing epistemic subjects, and to identify the qualities that characterize those agents who are doing best in epistemic pursuits, as well as offering ways of explaining concepts such as knowledge and justification.[26] They often focus on the qualities of a believer or epistemic subject in order to explain or define some valued epistemic state such as knowledge or justifiedness. Intellectual virtues are qualities and abilities that we value and encourage, and the reasons and motivations for such valuation are not limited to the desire for truth. Qualities such as honesty and trustworthiness are already part of the vocabulary of (moral) virtue theory, so it might seem likely that epistemic virtue theorists would be in the forefront of discussions of communal epistemic practices. However, virtue epistemologists often retain an individualistic focus, and this, not surprisingly, has limited their contribution to understanding epistemic interdependence.

In fact, individualism and a focus on knowledge increase are endemic in virtue epistemology. The most often discussed epistemic virtues are those suited to intellectual pursuits and new discoveries. These would be useful, for example, for an individual scientist proposing and testing hypotheses, or perhaps for a philosopher devising arguments.[27] The account I develop explores the virtues of epistemic agents who are not merely knowledge seekers and collectors, but interdependent members of epistemic communities.[28] Such epistemic agents are concerned with much more than knowledge increase—we do more than know and tell. We also are concerned with how we go about collective projects of inquiry and discovery, and with how other epistemic agents are dealt with along the way.

It might seem that a concern with how other agents are dealt with brings the discussion away from epistemology and into the domain of ethics or politics. This is correct insofar as there are often ethical and political dimensions to how others are dealt with in knowledge related transactions, but not insofar as it presumes that philosophical attention to dealings with other agents entails a departure from epistemology. As the above discussion shows, dependence is integral to epistemic activity, and it is not a matter of treating others as instruments or as data containers. For now, I am taking up topics and resources that are already acknowledged as part of the epistemic domain, without insisting on a sharp division between these concerns and those of ethics and politics of social justice.

Participating in an epistemic community is valuable for epistemic agents, but this participation is not restricted to being exposed to the information others make available, nor is its value reducible to the value of knowledge increase. Knowledge increase does not exhaust the domain of epistemic value. Being trusted and treated as credible is good for me as an epistemic agent, although it does not always mean that I know any more. Being excluded, dismissed, having my epistemic authority undermined or denied need not reduce my knowledge, or the knowledge of those around me, but it is an epistemic harm to me, it diminishes my epistemic agency. The full range of epistemic goods includes those that derive from the quality and sustainability of the epistemic community, from patterns of participation of is members, from its openness to critical reflection, from the richness of roles available to all agents in the arrangement of division of epistemic labor. Epistemically responsible agents need to attend to all these things, and responsible epistemologists should not ignore them.

COMMUNAL VIRTUES

Having argued for the importance of epistemic dependence, I turn to two contrasting appeals to the epistemic community to explicate intellectual virtues or duties. In her work on feminist intellectual virtue, Jane Braaten articulates a concern with thinkers as members of existing communities and as builders of future communities.[29] Following an explication of her work, and its application to epistemic communities, I criticize a very thin account of epistemic community that is used in a description of epistemic duty. I show that this account does not suffice even for its own stated purposes.

Jane Braaten analyses the virtues required of members who participate in sustainability, maintenance, and construction of communities, and her account is applicable to epistemic communities as well as to the social and political domain where her focus lies. Epistemic agency requires a social environment for reasons of practical necessity (such as the division of epistemic labor) and because it is a normative environment where standards are learned and maintained communally.[30] A concern for intellectual traits has to include a concern for the social environments that develop and sustain such characteristics. This is a useful way to approach thinking about epistemic communities where members not only share information, but also act as exemplars, cooperators, trainers, and teachers, and in doing so often reflect critically on epistemic practices.

Braaten examines the kind of intelligence manifested in building community and relationships. She joins a challenge to the historically dominant view that takes intelligence to be quantifiable by psychometric tests of skills like mathematical reasoning. These tests give a ranking to examinees according to their performance on highly abstract tasks like the recognition of patterns in series of numbers. According to Braaten, intellectual virtues are better understood as those conducive to the kind of thinking exercised in creating "an environment in which all members of the community have the opportunity to live well."[31] Braaten leaves the details of a good society fairly open, but necessary changes would include the avoidance of racist, coercive, and sexist social structures.[32] The virtues she describes are highly complex learned abilities that would permit such transformations, which are possible because we (the members of a community) are responsible for choosing which characteristics to foster and value. The aim of social transformation does not require an account of essential human nature, but of social justice, and this need not be a static ideal: "A society decides what it is to be intelligent when it decides that high school students should turn into the sort of persons who can do calculus and creative writing rather than the sort of persons who can hunt game, tell stories, or raise a child."[33]

Now for a society to survive, raising children must be an ability learned to an adequate degree and practiced by a sufficient number of members, so a society cannot really decide to abandon that practice. But there are choices about how to undertake the practice, and Braaten shows that such choices will reflect and perhaps determine whether relevant skills and traits count as intelligence. Importantly for my purposes, she includes the capacity to reflect on social conditions as part of the range of intellectual virtues. "The third [ability constitutive of intellectual virtue] is an abstractive ability, namely the ability to recognize social norms and values as socially constructed, rather than as a priori truths."[34] The virtue Braaten identifies with respect to social justice is also present in epistemological evaluation. We need to be able to consider whether a particular standard of justification is appropriate to a given context—perhaps I can justifiedly believe a stranger's advice about the location of the post office, but less plausibly their advice about taxation law. This is different from the introspection required for critical reflection on my own beliefs—it is relevant to others' practices not just my own, and to be virtuous, I need to be responsive when others raise justificatory standards, not just reflective about my own. I will argue below that considerations of reliability are not the only ones at stake in such transactions. In order to be a full member of an epistemic community, I need to be able to negotiate a variety of roles, involving not just exchanges of information, but exchanges of reasons, and require complex skills of navigating different ways of dependence and dependability.

Braaten does not see truth and increasing knowledge as the aim of intellectually virtuous effort. Rather, such efforts can be directed to social change, altering the conditions under which members of a community live. The success of such efforts, and the relevant virtues, cannot be assessed by the right/wrong, true/false standards applied in many tests of intelligence. Like others in psychology and education theory, Braaten advocates a transformation "of the prevailing presumptions about intelligence" to include "social intelligence."[35] Again, we can see the parallel between her approach to thinking about a political community and my account of an epistemic community. Relevant abilities include "an imaginative ability: the ability to represent alternative subjective points of view" and "an inductive ability to hypothesize about the sources of discord and wellbeing, both in personal and interpersonal affairs."[36] Braaten's intellectual virtues include a desire to understand and engage with other knowers, and to respect and acknowledge others. As a result, an intellectually virtuous person in Braaten's terms is markedly different from one who is motivated solely by a desire for truth and understanding.

Whether or not we share Braaten's concern for feminist political transformation, we can evaluate whether, and to what extent an epistemic community is conducive to Braaten's kind of reflective enterprise. Instead of focusing exclusively on increasing human knowledge, or scientific advances, we might also ask whether all a community's members have opportunities to think well, to learn and to teach, to defer and to be authoritative, to trust and to be trusted. We might ask whether everyone is allowed to navigate a range of roles and to assist in the direction of inquiry, in the construction, not just the acquisition of knowledge. To what extent does the community promote and preserve epistemic justice?

Braaten plausibly claims that imaginative and creative thinking about future social arrangements is an important intellectual process, which intellectually virtuous persons ought to be well equipped to undertake. Likewise, thinking about the current and future state of our epistemic community is part of epistemic responsibility. This is not to say that every epistemic agent must undertake this work, rather, that it is part of the range of tasks that members of an epistemic community collectively need to cover, and which are the proper domain of epistemological inquiry.

In contrast to this rich and complex view of epistemic value, many accounts within traditional epistemology present a single standard for evaluation of epistemic practice. Alvin Goldman is fairly typical in his endorsement of "veritism," a position in which the main epistemic goal is increase of true belief—a rough stand-in for knowledge. In *Knowledge in a Social World* and earlier work on epistemic paternalism[37] Goldman investigates the conditions under which policies have "good or bad epistemic consequences: i.e., good *veritistic* outcomes."[38] His view is thus a kind of consequentialism in which the good result to be promoted consists in increasing true beliefs. Goldman canvasses a range of ways that veritistic improvements can arise. For example, fecundity—the number of people acquiring true beliefs—may increase, although this may require a simplification that involves the omission of some truths. Avoiding error and confusion can likewise compensate for some truth omissions, in at least some cases.[39]

Knowledge increase is at best an ambiguous standard when applied to a community, as Goldman acknowledges. New discoveries must count, but is novelty commensurate with dissemination, or with access and participation? Each of these is an important aspect of an epistemic community and arguably each can be related to knowledge increase, but it is not clear that we could or should compare them to one another. Increasing the education levels of a community, increasing research productivity, and increasing the number and diversity of people involved in research and education projects produce more true beliefs in different ways, and there are multiple ways of evaluating a community of epistemic agents engaged in diverse practices. In addition to veritism, we might appeal to sustainability, inclusiveness, and participation, or the avoidance of various forms of epistemic injustice. Goldman specifically includes fecundity—the number of people acquiring true beliefs—as an epistemic gain. And it would seem that there are multiple ways for agents to contribute to each of these good aspects of community. Before turning to some accounts of these communally focused virtues, it is useful to show that veritism, even with the multiple aspects that Goldman describes, does not provide a clear or an adequate goal for a community of epistemic agents. A broader or more complex account of epistemic value is called for.

The tendency of epistemologists to take too narrow a view of the scope of epistemic virtue (by limiting it to just what is conducive to knowledge increase, or veritism) has not only neglected important epistemic virtues but has left the epistemic community under-theorized. The following example shows how, if the account of epistemic community is too narrow, epistemological analysis tends to go wrong.

Richard Hall and Charles Johnson[40] appeal directly to "the community" as they derive specific epistemic duties from the goal of believing all and only truths.[41] They suggest that in selecting my epistemic projects, I should direct my efforts with reference to the true beliefs of the community, not just my individual situation. Thus, "if other competent investigators are already investigating *s*, then by gathering evidence on *p*, *q*, and *r* rather than *s*, you help the whole community closer to the goal."[42] The epistemic goal of believing truly is, therefore, not to be cashed out in purely individual terms.

The claim that as a member of the epistemic community, I should consider others' activities is surely right. But Hall and Johnson don't pursue the implications of their claim far enough. Presumably, when I take into account the activities of others, I am entitled to suppose that the evidence they acquire will be available to me and that I can rely on it without checking for myself. Otherwise there is no benefit to me, and conversely, my evidence seeking would be irrelevant to others. I need access to others' knowledge for it to be in my epistemic interests (taken in Hall and Johnson's own terms as comprising the goal of believing all and only truths) to avoid duplicating others' evidence seeking.[43] If I cannot acquire others' knowledge without further evidence, then it is not clear that I ought to take their knowledge-seeking activities into account. In such circumstances, it would make no difference to me that others are already investigating *s*.

Noticing that unless information is shared, it would make no sense for one individual or group to avoid duplicating others' investigations has practical as well as theoretical implications. Consider exchanges (or notoriously problematic lack of exchanges) between government departments charged with protecting a community from terrorist organizations. "Need to know" and "need to share" impose quite different obligations on agents and agencies.

Hall and Johnson's advice to avoid duplicating others' investigations entails that I can acquire knowledge from others without needing to seek further evidence. In other words, it implies trust is a source of knowledge distinct from evidence seeking. While I think this is correct, and I will discuss trust in more detail in the next chapter, this recognition complicates the goal that Hall and Johnson endorse and the duty they derive. If I can acquire others' knowledge without seeking further evidence (that is, via trust and testimony), then the epistemic goal of believing all and only truths might dictate different duties: for example, rather than investigate as Christopher does, perhaps I ought to seek persons to believe, and follow Dennis' example. Bringing the community closer to the goal seems likely to require not only carefully directed investigation, but also strategies for disseminating information. The relevant epistemic duties are plural and complex, even within the terms of an appeal to a common goal of increasing knowledge.

When Hall and Johnson present a division of epistemic labor in which each agent has a duty to investigate matters that others are not pursuing, they seem to treat the knowledge each agent acquires from others as potentially equivalent to that which she obtains by her own efforts. The above discussions show that taking interdependence seriously is not just a matter of expanding a list of virtues with a passing nod to non-individualistic concepts such as community or human knowledge. It also means recognizing the complex practices of interdependence that are not reducible to acquiring knowledge as getting the right, justified answers, or the accumulation of individually exercised competences.

In the original Dennis and Christopher example, as in Hall and Johnson's discussion, social differences that could problematize impeccable transmission of information between the parties are not considered. Ideal epistemic agents are abstracted from concrete social circumstances in order to focus on pure transmission. Lisa A. Bergin criticizes this idea of transmission, and contrasts the idea of epistemic difference with the idea that knowledge can be acquired by anyone. Rather, she claims epistemic difference means that "knowledge has to be connected to a particular point of view"[44] and social differences have to be negotiated. Bergin recommends that "transmission" models are replaced with a "dialogue/relationship in which both participants reflect on the epistemic differences that exist between themselves."[45] She presents a more complex and more deeply social account of epistemic dependence than those of Zagzebski, Kvanvig, or Hall and Johnson. There are some relatively uncomplicated testimonial exchanges (like asking a colleague for the time), but others, such as the ethnographic examples Bergin explores, cannot be explained as simple one-way provision or transmission of information.

This chapter demonstrates that there are multiple ways of evaluating an epistemic community and the practices within it. The comparison of Dennis and Christopher shows at least that the denigration of dependence in contrast to independent investigation is a mistake and suggests the range of epistemic virtues relevant to testimonial transactions is wider than many epistemologists have recognized. This broader account emerges from a close examination of epistemic dependence. It is a mistake to take information sharing or transmission as exhausting the forms of epistemic dependence.[46] The epistemic community is not only the environment in which a great deal of knowledge is acquired, but is also necessary for cultivating other important dimensions of epistemic agency such as recognizing appropriate authorities, responding to justificatory demands, and maintaining or revising epistemic standards. Two common errors have been exposed: one is to assume the superiority of independent ways of acquiring knowledge; the other is to neglect the complexity of epistemic interactions that are not reducible to knowledge transmissions. Within epistemic relationships, the proper motivation is not to seek and promote truth always and everywhere, nor even to maximize the amount of relevant truth one conveys to others. This gives a *prima facie* reason to think that ignorance is important because it is an ineliminable part of responsible engagement with other knowers. Having argued for the importance of explaining specific features of the epistemic community, I turn in the next chapter to a detailed analysis of two central forms of epistemic dependence: trust and testimony. There, I begin to explain the role of ignorance in epistemic practices. Beyond collecting, accumulating and passing on information, epistemic agents negotiate status, justification, norms, standards, recognition, credit, and acknowledgement. Epistemic values include the sustainability of the community, acknowledgment, recognition of others' authority, respect, and epistemic justice. An explanation of the value of these practices includes an account of the roles and functions of ignorance because their value is not reducible to increasing knowledge. Extending the range of concerns beyond increasing knowledge motivates, for example, careful attention to the role of disclosers, not just receivers of testimony. An adequate account of epistemic virtues answers such questions as: what makes a community member a good epistemic co-operator as well as an effective collector and distributor of knowledge?

NOTES

1. Charles Dickens, *Hard Times* (Harmondsworth: Penguin, 1995), 9. I thank Philippa Byers for this reference.
2. Edward Craig, *Knowledge and the State of Nature: An Essay in Conceptual Synthesis* (Oxford: Oxford University Press, 1990).
3. For example, by developing a set of necessary and sufficient conditions that is immune to the proliferation of Gettier-type cases.
4. See Lorraine Code, *Epistemic Responsibility* (Hanover and London: University Press of New England, 1987); Lorraine Code, *What Can She Know?* (Ithaca and London: Cornell University Press, 1991); Code, *Rhetorical Spaces*; and Code, *Ecological Thinking*. In these books Lorraine Code contrasts an epistemology committed to relationality (in *Ecological Thinking* she uses the term "cohabitability") with the tradition of individualism that is dominant in epistemology. This kind of account which emphasises persons who know, and the diversity of significant epistemic relationships, has the resources for an account of epistemic trust, and it is from such an account that the crucial functions of ignorance become apparent.
5. Fricker, "Powerlessness and Social Interpretation," 96–108; Fricker, *Epistemic Injustice*.
6. Jonathan Kvanvig, *The Intellectual Virtues and the Life of the Mind.* (Savage: Rowman and Littlefield, 1992), 148. In my discussion I will use Zagzebski's characters, but the points apply equally well to Kvanvig's S1 and S2.
7. Zagzebski, *Virtues of the Mind*, 26–27. Her source is Charles Taliaferro, "Divine Cognitive Power," *International Journal of Philosophy of Religion* 18 (1985): 133–40. As I am interested in ordinary knowers, not the omniscience of interest to Taliaferro, I will not discuss his argument directly.
8. Zagzebski, *Virtues of the Mind*, 27. At this point in her discussion Zagzebski has transformed the initial thought experiment into one involving ordinary human knowledge rather than the omniscience that interests Taliaferro.
9. . Lorraine Code's term.
10. Originally, the term "computer" referred to human agents who performed calculations, but it is clearly the machine sense that Zagzebski has in mind.
11. Both Zagzebski and Kvanvig present their examples in a way that suggests the entire cognitive worth of the participants is at issue. It is, I think, more plausible that just these practices should be evaluated, and that an assessment of the cognitive worth of a character would be much more complicated, if possible at all. I think the names are used as a stand-in for the practices. (I thank an anonymous reader for encouraging this clarification.)

12. A related point is made in Lisa A. Bergin's rich discussion of testimony. She shows that "although often hidden, the receiver's active role is present in all knowledge communication." Lisa A. Bergin, "Testimony, epistemic difference, and privilege: How feminist epistemology can improve our understanding of the communication of knowledge," *Social Epistemology* 16: 3 (2002): 209.

13. Later, a richer and more complex notion of responsibility will be developed, but for the moment I am assuming that acquiring true beliefs can indicate responsibility. This is compatible with Zagzebski's insistence that epistemic virtues are necessarily truth-conducive, which I accept here for the sake of argument.

14. Goldman comments that "BLIND TRUST [to believe every piece of testimony you hear] is an excellent acceptance practice if it complements a reporting practice that generates only truths," Goldman, *Knowledge in a Social World*, 109. He would therefore, I think, admit Dennis' practice as excellent within this example, but as Goldman notes, such an ideal environment is not a realistic prospect.

15. Miranda Fricker's *Epistemic Injustice* is more concerned with obstacles such as identity prejudice faced by testifiers, but her discussion also shows clearly how hard it can be to be a responsible hearer of testimony.

16. Peter Graham suggests that testimony has perhaps been seen as controversial because it involves another's agency, in Peter Graham, "Testimony, Agency and Entitlement" (paper presented at the Southern California Philosophy Conference, Irvine, California, September 27, 2001). He argues, I think rightly, this is not a reason to dismiss testimony.

17. . See also Tony Coady's discussion of the disappearance of history in C. A. J. Coady, *Testimony* (Oxford: Clarendon Press, 1992), 199–223.

18. I am not claiming that objectification of persons is morally inappropriate, like the Kantian characterization of treating others as means, although I think that it is so. Nor am I denying that there are moral concerns in teaching and medical disclosure.

19. Compare Edward Craig's discussion of sources and informants. For Craig, it is important that epistemic agents are treated as participants in the epistemic community, rather than mere objects or sources, but his focus is on the agent's contribution to knowledge increase, whereas I see participation in the epistemic community as involving a much wider range of activities. Craig, *Knowledge and the State of Nature*, see especially 35–44.

20. Dickens satirizes this approach to education: "The speaker, and the schoolmaster, and the third grown person present, all backed a little, and swept with their eyes the inclined plane of little vessels, then and there arranged in order, ready to have imperial gallons of facts poured into them until they were full to the brim." Dickens, *Hard Times*, 9.

21. Christopher Hookway discusses a teacher's "failure to respect a student as a potential contributor to discussion" (due to prejudice against the student) as a case of epistemic injustice. Christopher Hookway, "Some Varieties of Epistemic Injustice: Reflections on Fricker," *Episteme* 7 (2010): 151–63. A system to mark students' written work anonymously is an example of indirect mitigation of such bias. It does not directly address the teacher's failure to respect the student, nor would it remedy the negative effects of such in-class treatment, but it would mean that the student received appropriate credit in another context, and might also help the teacher to revise her or his preconceptions of the student's capacities.

22. Dale Spender documents research showing this has been a common way of treating girls and boys differently in classrooms. Dale Spender, *Invisible Women: The Schooling Scandal* (London: Writers and Readers, 1982).

23. Edward Craig contrasts persons as a source of information and informants, although his concern is the success of inquiry, not epistemic virtue as it pertains to the treatment of others in an epistemic community.

24. Further argument will show that one who provides information to another has an *epistemic* not merely an ethical responsibility to consider the way that the information is transferred. The claim at this stage is that being in a position of epistemic dependence does not equate to cognitive inferiority.

25. Zagzebski explains her project as follows: "in *Virtues of the Mind* . . . I am giving a theory of *human* knowledge, not an analysis of the *concept* of knowledge." Linda Zagzebski, "Responses," *Philosophy and Phenomenological Research* LX: 1 (2000): 209.

26. Linda Zagzebski, for example, suggests that a virtue based epistemology "permits a wider range of epistemic evaluation than that which focuses exclusively on properties of individual belief states." Zagzebski, *Virtues of the Mind*, 274. Alvin Goldman suggests as a "rough" account that: "Beliefs acquired (or retained) through a chain of 'virtuous' psychological processes qualify as justified; those acquired partly through cognitive 'vices' are derogated as unjustified." Alvin Goldman, "Epistemic Folkways and Scientific Epistemology," in *Readings in Philosophy and Cognitive Science,* ed. A. Goldman (Cambridge, Massachusetts: MIT Press, 1993), 97.

27. But some explorations of virtues are not limited to such individual pursuits of knowledge. Feminist approaches in particular are notable for attention to interdependence. For example, in Lorraine Code's analysis, it is crucial that the epistemic agents in question are social beings treating one another as second persons. Code, *Epistemic Responsibility*.

28. The main distinction within virtue epistemology is not between individualist and communalist approaches, but between reliabilism and responsibilism. See for example, Axtell, "Recent Work on Virtue Epistemology," 1–26.

29. Jane Braaten, "Towards a Feminist Reassessment of Intellectual Virtue," *Hypatia* 5, no. 3 (1990): 1–14.

30. Academics' roles are not limited to pursuing their own research and discoveries, we also have to contribute to educating the new generation of experts, and to the institutional structure that enables these enterprises. If the university is an epistemic community, then sustaining its existence not only via transmission of knowledge, but also enculturation of virtues, training of skills and the like is epistemic work.

31. Braaten, "A Feminist Reassessment," 5. In this way, the goal of Braaten's feminist intellectual virtue is like Aristotelian *eudaimonia* or flourishing, but this similarity should not be overemphasised since Aristotle bases his understanding of virtue in an account of human nature. The *telos* for Braaten is inherently cultural and constructed, neither innate nor individualistic, since it is the transformation of society that is the aim.

32. Braaten, "A Feminist Reassessment," 13.

33. Braaten, "A Feminist Reassessment," 4. Of course, for any society to survive there must be resources for childrearing. But seeing these as forms of intelligence, to be cultivated and valued like western societies cultivate and value literacy is a radical suggestion.

34. . Braaten, "A Feminist Reassessment," 6.

35. Braaten, "A Feminist Reassessment," 4.

36. Braaten, "A Feminist Reassessment," 6.

37. Alvin Goldman, "Epistemic Paternalism: Communication Control in Law and Society," *The Journal of Philosophy* 88: 3 (1991): 113–131.

38. Goldman, "Epistemic Paternalism," 124.

39. Goldman, "Epistemic Paternalism," 123.

40. Richard J. Hall and Charles R. Johnson, "The Epistemic Duty to Seek More Evidence," *American Philosophical Quarterly* 35: 2 (1998): 129–39.

41. I also disagree with their endorsement of the common claim that there is one overarching epistemic goal, that of believing all and only truths. While I don't deny that believing truths is an epistemic good, it is not the only one.

42. Hall and Johnson, "The Epistemic Duty," 134.

43. In fact, there can be very good reasons to duplicate others' evidence seeking, such as corroboration, repetition of scientific experimentation, learning and practicing techniques, following in the footsteps of an exemplar and so on.

44. Bergin, "Testimony, epistemic difference and privilege," 201.

45. Bergin, "Testimony, epistemic difference and privilege," 209.

46. There are a number of epistemologists who are working on these questions. Social epistemology is a significant move away from the traditional individualism, and feminist theorists are primary sources of critiques of old-style epistemology, although not all such comments are generated by specifically feminist concerns. For example, the following comment is found in M. O. Webb, "Why I Know About As Much As You: A Reply to Hardwig," *The Journal of Philosophy* 90: 5 (1993): 270: "If I am right about the dependence of knowledge generally on trust, then all knowledge (except perhaps primitive perceptual knowledge) is as essentially

social as science is. . . . This possibility raises several new questions, including how our analysis of epistemic concepts should be affected, what happens to the skeptical challenge, and whether epistemic and doxastic practices can rightly be criticised on moral and political grounds." Jonathan Kvanvig also comments on what he terms the Cartesian perspective criticising "disturbing aspects of recent epistemological inquiry—aspects signaled by charges of irrelevance to the cognitive life and interminability of debate." Kvanvig, *The Intellectual Virtues*, 187. But these concerns are not yet mainstream, and much of this work is revisionary and often marginalised as "non standard."

Chapter Two

Ignorance and the Interdependence of Epistemic Agents

Epistemic practice is deeply cooperative. To cooperate well with her fellows, a member of an epistemic community needs at least a tacit understanding of the value of ignorance. Possession of ignorance that the agent does not seek to eliminate, and practical competence with respect to if and how to remedy others' ignorance are both part of communal epistemic life. The values expressed by interdependent epistemic agents are not reducible to the value of increasing knowledge for oneself or for others. The practices of epistemic agents are not reducible to the activities of acquiring and transmitting information. Having shown in chapter 1 that epistemic dependence is not inferior to knowledge acquisition, I here explore that dependence in more detail, and will show that there are two distinct mechanisms of dependence on others' testimony: reliance and trust. Both are important, and trust ineliminably involves ignorance in its simple form of lacking knowledge, and refraining from remedying that lack.

I discuss trust in detail because it provides a clear case of epistemic dependence in which the values are not reducible to simple knowledge increase. To make this clear, I first distinguish trust from reliance, and defend a particular account of trust as a commitment. This account of trust contrasts with others taking it to be an affective attitude, and I will compare the commitment and affective analyses of betrayal and the eliciting of trust. I consider the gullibility objection to trust and cases where trust is problematic. The predicament of mythological character Cassandra is used to illustrate the non-veritistic value of being trusted, and finally I explore Miranda Fricker's discussion of epistemic injustice which shows up the importance of credibility and credence—of being acknowledged as a reliable or trusted interlocutor.

Trust is an indispensable source of knowledge, but its value is not purely instrumental. The distinction between trust and reliance aligns with the difference between relationships of epistemic dependence in which an epistemic participant must be understood as a credible agent or can be reduced to a reliable instrument. In trusting, we treat our epistemic fellows non-instrumentally, and this forms the foundation for the wider epistemic virtues of acknowledgment and epistemic respect, whose counterpart vices are discredit and disrespect. Ignorance is inherent in trust, hence ineliminably part of these virtuous dimensions of epistemic agency.

In practice, epistemic agents frequently treat ignorance as a state that need not, or ought not be remedied. Sometimes this is because other information is more important, so this information is foregone or subordinated to matters of increasing information elsewhere or there is a trade off between fecundity and more people acquiring simpler beliefs and beliefs of greater depth. Other motives are not so benign.[1] Some epistemologists, such as Alvin Goldman, have acknowledged that some level of ignorance (understood as the result of paternalistic withholding or omitting of some truths[2]) can be tolerated in some instances. But this concession retains a negative conception of ignorance—all things being equal, it should be eliminated. Seeing the non-instrumental function of trust which is partially constituted by ignorance leads to a reassessment of this devaluation. A state of ignorance in an epistemic agent need not be evaluated negatively nor seen as second-best, but instead as part of a positive and necessary form of epistemic dependence.

Connections between trust, secrecy, and confidentiality are not coincidental. All involve forbearance to investigate or disclose, that is, the avoidance of an increase of knowledge. Trust includes restraint from the side of a person we trust with information: she will keep our secrets, which suggests that she will believe them as well as not betray them. Trust also involves restraint from the trustor's side. I will show that trust has the structure of forbearing to acquire information, because it is, among other things, a commitment not to check up on the trusted party. And trust is, as well as an irreplaceable source of information, a necessary condition for fostering virtues of epistemic community and for avoiding what Miranda Fricker calls "a distinctively epistemic kind of oppression."[3] Forbearing to acquire information when pursuing information would undermine epistemic relationships can be epistemically admirable, but need not meet a veritistic standard nor yield net knowledge increase.

Trust and some epistemic virtues are antithetical to collecting or disseminating maximal knowledge. Most obviously, selectivity requires excluding irrelevant, dangerous, or destructive knowledge. Irrelevant true information may be misleading and distracting as authors and readers of detective stories know well. Even if information is relevant, it might not help the recipient who is flooded with too much, and may lack the resources to deal with it.[4]

Providing too much information means that what is transferred is likely swamped and less useful to the recipient. Just as, if we are cooperating, we should organize information suitably for the recipient, we present it in some order, and we typically restrict what is communicated so what is important stands out. This kind of selectivity is explicable as managing ignorance just as well as managing knowledge. Discretion also involves ignorance as in selecting whom and how much I inform, I consider what another person should not or need not know—the scope of their ignorance.

Abandoning the form of epistemophilia that mandates knowledge increase as the only epistemic good means that the temptation for agents to figure in epistemology merely as instruments and sources of knowledge, or opportunities to improve veritistic outcomes is dispelled. It becomes much easier to see that epistemic agents are more than spectators, collectors, and transmitters of information. Critiques along these lines have been presented by feminist epistemologists who tend to start from looking at the actual patterns of knowledge interactions with a concern to identify and contest those patterns that support subordinations and oppressions on the basis of gender or other social group difference. For now, I want to focus on the epistemic side of these practices and will return to the ethical and political questions. My argument shows that even on epistemic terms, a spectator-collector-transmitter model of virtuous epistemic agency is inadequate.

Seeing oneself as nothing more than a collector/sharer of knowledge inhibits the capacity to reflect on dimensions of epistemic practice, such as the background social conditions that construct patterns of credibility and authority, from the epistemic side. Epistemophilia does not encourage a full understanding of epistemic responsibility, of what I should do precisely as an agent concerned with knowledge, in either a personal or professional capacity. Ignorance is important to the ways we reflect on our epistemic activities and contributions. If we don't opt for optimizing knowledge we are tolerating, endorsing, or accepting ignorance that we could, but choose not, to remedy. Yet an over-valuation of knowledge can be combined with an invested ignorance, and can impede a critical attitude to that ignorance. Epistemic practice and reflecting on that practice both demand that ignorance is taken seriously.

Understanding ignorance improves the understanding of interactions taking place between agents who are, among other things, able to trust and to be trusted. I will examine trust and reliance here, the less formal kinds of epistemic dependence, and in the following chapter explore the division of epistemic labor in which epistemic dependence can be institutionalized. I will show that trust is a form of epistemic dependence that, in at least some of its forms, irreducibly involves ignorance and that it is ineliminable from a flourishing epistemic community. Thus, any epistemic framework that implies the elimination of ignorance is always a good should be revised.

TRUST AND RELIANCE

Trust has an extensive role in the network of relations that constitutes an epistemic community. It is central to epistemic cooperation, within and beyond the sphere of testimonial dependence (dependence on testimony for acquiring knowledge). Both trust and reliance enable the acquisition of knowledge, but trust does more than this.[5] Trust serves both to facilitate exchanges of knowledge and to maintain cooperative relationships. Trust involves commitment and reciprocal responsibility, and an epistemic community is partially constituted by commitments not to breach trust. In various forms of transaction, members of epistemic communities acknowledge one another, assign credibility, and make epistemic authority manifest by acting on such assignments.[6] Relationships of epistemic dependence also form the background for establishing and maintaining cooperative standards.

Trust involves virtues and competences that are not reducible to the risk assessment grounds of reliability judgments. When I rely on, but do not trust another, I can regard them just as an instrument in my belief formation. I may treat the interaction merely as a judgment about the risk and probability associated with believing what they tell me. Some discussions of testimony and epistemic dependence such as those of Alvin Goldman and Jonathan Adler focus on reliability of (human) instruments,[7] but such accounts ignore how trust differs from reliance. The discrimination involved in trust is not merely a belief (or set of beliefs) about a person's report or judgment of her character. Trust is based on seeing another as a second person, and it entails at least tacit acknowledgment that one is dealing an epistemic agent not just an instrument,[8] in a relationship which can be damaged by the trustor as well as the trustee, and by disbelief as well as by suspicion. Such recognition is not reducible to a belief about the other party; rather, trustful engagement requires that the trustor constrain her own conduct in appropriate ways. Although some theorists consider trust to parallel gullibility in critical respects, in fact, trust involves skills, judgment, and discrimination, which can be exercised more or less wisely and well.

My discussion of trust is not exhaustive. In my view, trust and distrust can both vary on multiple dimensions, although there isn't scope to develop this idea fully here.[9] While trust is not monolithic, nor are trust and distrust always simple opposites, such that the presence of one signifies the absence of the other. Some of the examples below are somewhat simplified and simply bracket the possibilities of mixed trust and distrust, in order to focus on and highlight the role of ignorance. And here, it is simple ignorance—lack of knowledge that could be remedied—that is most salient.[10]

Trustful engagements impose standards and expectations beyond the requirement that one person report sincerely and accurately and another be justified in recognizing this. This is sufficient for successful reliance, but not for trust. In trusting you, I expect not just that you wouldn't lie to me, but that you wouldn't be the first to breach our relationship, and in trusting you, I reciprocally undertake to uphold my side of the trustful engagement. Accepting this account of trust requires renouncing evidentialism (the claim that beliefs should always be based in evidence), but there is a significant gain in explanatory power.

Ignorance is embedded in the structure of trust. Epistemic trust restricts what I can do with respect to evidence and justification. If the trusting person is committed to believing the person she trusts, her trust obliges her to refrain from double-checking. The tacit acknowledgment that further evidence could, but in fact will not be, obtained means that a degree of ignorance is willfully maintained. As a result, trust is problematic for accounts of epistemic virtue (or any way in which ideal practice is cashed out) that require evidential gaps to be filled in so that ignorance is eliminated or minimized. The problem arises because one central meaning of trust is that I take you at your word: insofar as I trust, I cannot keep checking to confirm or corroborate what you have told me; I cannot seek alternative sources to replace or bolster my confidence in you. In other contexts, it may be that a degree of trust leads me to investigate, and without that minimal level of credibility I would simply dismiss a claim. Here, it would be trust, rather than distrust that leads to further inquiry and seeking of evidence.[11] In the first kind of case, however, trust requires that certain opportunities for knowledge or increased certainty are foregone and certain kinds or domains of ignorance must be accepted, even maintained, in order for the very possibility of trust to obtain. Ignorance, then, is not only necessary for generating the need for trust, it is sometimes indispensable for maintaining the conditions of manifest trust.

Two of the main ways that ignorance is related to trust are therefore, firstly, that trust is a way to overcome ignorance, that is, a way to obtain knowledge. It seems straightforward that if I can legitimately trust someone who is a potential source of knowledge then I may be able to move from ignorance to knowledge.[12] Secondly, trust may preclude certain kinds of checking, as they are incompatible with a trustful attitude. This second way that ignorance and trust are related shows that trust can be distinguished from mere reliance by its different configurations of evidence and judgment. Without this distinction, the extended role and value of trust are both obscured.

An example makes it clear that trust can be a commitment that involves ignorance. Consider a scenario presented by Jack Meiland: "Take the classical case in which a wife finds a blonde hair on her husband's coat, a handkerchief with lipstick on it in his pocket, a scrap of paper with a phone number scrawled on it, and so on."[13]

Suppose Emily encounters such a situation, is aware of what this evidence could imply,[14] and asks for and receives an explanation from her partner

Henry—his story is more or less believable.[15] Later, she describes the incident to a friend, Ingrid, who responds: "Well, you know I have just completed my private investigator training. I could find out whether he is up to something." Emily's acceptance of such an offer would indicate a lack of trust in Henry. Although she did not manifest *maximally* distrustful behavior, for example, she did not seek out someone to spy on Henry, if she were to accept her friend's offer to investigate, he could justifiably accuse her of not trusting him. (Again, it does not matter if he is or is pretending to be innocent. That affects the wisdom or foolishness of her trust, but is not relevant to whether she is properly characterized as trusting.)

Emily might refuse Ingrid's offer, because she trusts Henry. According to some accounts that will be discussed below, this means she has a positive affective attitude towards him. In this context, she has a distinctive way of seeing him, and a tendency to interpret the situation accordingly. But this attitude is not enough. What if Wendy, similarly situated, with the same emotional attitudes (to her partner Harry, to the credibility of his story and so on) is also compliant and easily led? Her detective friend Betty persuades her to endorse the investigation, and Wendy gives in, not because her attitude to Harry has changed, but because it is overridden. Resistance is too hard and she succumbs to Betty's persuasive and forceful character. Trust, I'll argue, involves a commitment, and an emotional attitude without this commitment does not add up to trust. If Wendy fails to live up to such a commitment, she is properly charged with distrust.

We can schematize the cases I have described in the following way:

1. Right affect[16] plus robust disposition plus temptation to check up—no distrustful act (Emily);
2. Right affect plus compliant disposition plus temptation to check up—distrustful act (Wendy).

Emily is *prima facie* trusting, Wendy is not. This suggests that what makes the difference here is the constraint on conduct, which I have called commitment, in this case a refusal to check up on a partner, even when the opportunity is made easy. Before leaving this example, consider two other possibilities:

3. Right affect absent plus temptation to check up—distrustful act.

This would apply to an agent who employed an investigator without hesitation. An agent described this way would not count as trusting on any of the accounts under consideration. A fourth case is more challenging for my account.

4. Right affect absent (replaced by apathy, indifference, distraction, laziness, or some other motive), plus temptation to check up—no distrustful act.

This possibility does not look like trust, which suggests that the presence of the right affect might be necessary after all, even if not sufficient for trust. I'll offer a different interpretation below. What characterizes cases of trust, I'll argue, is not feeling confident, nor possessing optimistic expectations, nor any similar affective attitude, but the trustor's preparedness to hold to a certain kind of commitment, whether this has been made explicit or not. Such a commitment constrains the trustor's behavior with respect to the investigations and the interpretations she can endorse. For example, as we have seen, she is precluded from some kinds of checking up on the one she claims to trust.

The account does not imply that the trustor must be foolish or oblivious, nor that trust requires her to give up responsible agency. Attending to evidence, and asking for reasons are up to a point compatible with trust. Trust does not eliminate critical faculties, but it does limit their exercise. Precisely what is ruled out depends on the context, but the constraints are not a matter of mere subjective judgment or determined by an individual's pattern of interpretation. Trust is a social practice and we can get an approximation of relevant limits by considering whether a claim that "you don't trust me" would be rationally justified. In the cases described above, if Harry were to learn of Wendy's endorsement of an investigation, he would be justified in accusing her of distrust.

Trust does not always mean a cessation of inquiry. Sometimes checking up is a signal of distrust. It means that a partner is not taken at his or her word, in a context where trust would require otherwise. In other kinds of case, say testimony about a surprising or unlikely event, I may be inclined to investigate further if the testifier was someone I trusted, but less so if it were someone I did not know, or who was known to be prone to exaggeration. The surprising testimony case would be followed up precisely because of a presumption in favor of the trusted person. Following up in the suspected infidelity case lacks such a presumption.[17] Trust however, always imposes constraints, often precluding some kinds of checking up or extra verification—responding to a surprising eye-witness report by requesting that the testifier have her eyes checked or undergo a drug scan, would (in many, if not most cases) be a kind of checking incompatible with trust.

If trust constrains the kinds of information or evidence that can be sought, then ignorance is inherent in trust. Below, I will compare this account directly with two versions of affective attitude accounts and show that it is better able to explain important phenomena related to trust, including the troublesome scenario 4.

BETRAYAL—MAKING SENSE OF AFFECT

The distinct ways that trust and reliance can fail show a clear difference between them: trustful cooperation between epistemic agents can be jeopardized by betrayal. It is only persons who can betray—machines and instruments can merely fail—and without a relationship of trust, persons too can only fail. In some relationships both are possible, in others, only failures of reliance can arise. If a member of the soccer team fails to kick a goal due to inadvertent inaccuracy, the consequences are different from those likely to arise if she is found to have done so deliberately, in order to throw the game. I might be irritated and inconvenienced if my car breaks down, but it is not a betrayal. Being untrustworthy is a form of failure that is not the same as being inaccurate, or even deceitful. Betrayal only occurs in the context of legitimate trustful expectations: if I deceive a person who expects me to be trying to trick her, she has not been betrayed. A magician does not betray the audience when they are persuaded that a coin placed in his mouth was then removed from his ear.

Only persons can respond or be unresponsive to my trust, in the sense of being motivated by their recognition of me as a person and as an epistemic agent to accept a responsibility or commitment with respect to me in this context. However, persons can be depended on without being trusted, and can respond reliably when, for example, a person whom I do not trust has an interest in correctly informing me on some occasion. Although my neighbor is usually evasive and misleading, this time she tells me where the best fresh fish can be obtained because she wants me to take her there. If I act on her advice, this is best characterized as reliance, rather than trust. So betrayal arises only in cases of trust, but betrayal concerns the response to trust, it does not explain what a person who trusts is doing.

The connection between betrayal and trust is sometimes taken to support the case for affective accounts of trust. It actually reflects the distinct sets of expectations that constitute the relation of trust and other forms of dependence. Betrayal occurs when trustful expectations are violated, not when there is just inconsistency, inaccuracy, or some other reason for failure. These expectations, I will now argue, are not defined by optimism or any other affective attitude,[18] but by a commitment not to breach trust either by distrust or by untrustworthiness.

It is undeniable that trust and emotion often go together, and certain accounts recognize, rightly, that there is more to trust than mere reliance or risk assessment.[19] But appreciating that trust and certain emotional or affective orientations often, perhaps usually, coincide should not lead us to adopt an affective account of trust, despite the initial appeal of such accounts.

The appeal of affective accounts of trust is evident in Karen Jones' account of trust, which combines affective and cognitive elements:

> trust is an attitude of optimism that the goodwill and competence of another will extend to cover the domain of our interaction with her, together with the expectation that the one trusted will be directly and favorably moved by the thought that we are counting on her. The attitude of optimism is to be cashed out not primarily in terms of beliefs about the other's trustworthiness, but rather—in accordance with certain contemporary accounts of the emotions [a footnote here refers to those of Rorty, Calhoun, and de Sousa]—in terms of a distinctive and affectively loaded way of seeing the one trusted. This way of seeing the other, with its constitutive patterns of attention and tendencies of interpretation, explains [various phenomena]. [20]

Similarly, Bernd Lahno describes trust as an emotional attitude that "lead[s] us to perceive and judge the world in a specific way."[21] Trust involves a participant attitude to the trusted person, seeing the other as a person responsible for her agency.[22] Trust differs from mere reliance because shared aims, norms, and values are ascribed to the trusted person. In cases of reliance, a person may depend on another without such an attitude or perspective: she may take a calculated risk, or undertake to rely in spite of believing the other person does not share any aims or values with her, for example, when this dependence is judged to be the best of available options.[23] Trust, in contrast, shapes the way we see the trusted person, and the way we interpret relevant facts and evidence related to that trustful context. According to Lahno, this emotionally charged perspective is distinctive of trust.[24]

Karen Jones' account of trust is similar. Like Lahno, she emphasizes that trust is not a mere belief about the other's goodwill; instead, trust is a ground for such beliefs, and indeed, Jones points out, trust can form the basis for beliefs that are abnormally resistant to evidence.[25] Both these attitudinists explicitly emphasize the forward looking nature of trust, and refer to the trustor's expectations of future responses and behavior from the one trusted. Both accounts, moreover, construe trust as seeing (an aspect of) the world in a particular way, as understanding evidence from this point of view. Specifically, trust requires me to see the person trusted as in some way opting to cooperate with me—having some discretion about how to act, and using that discretion to act in accord with, not against, my (the trustor's) interests.

Jones' and Lahno's accounts focus on the duties of a trusted person (obligations of trustworthiness) and on the trustor's concern for justification, and perhaps her duty to avoid gullibility. In these accounts, too much emphasis is placed on the trustor's expectations about the trusted person, and too little on the way that trust constrains the one who trusts. The trustor has a distinctive orientation to her own conduct in which trust-breaking acts are not available as options. Accounts that don't notice this commitment neglect this symmetrical aspect of trust: they obscure the fact that it can be breached from either side. Lahno compares trust with seeing the world through rose-colored glasses, but characterizing trust as an emotional attitude does not distinguish trust from other positive expectations that can structure our observations of evidence, such as wishful thinking. Merely having a positive attitude or rose-colored outlook need not involve any commitment to interpret future evidence in any particular way. To be sure, emotions play a causal role, inspiring trust, and even bolstering the commitment to maintain trust. My point is that these affective attitudes do not constitute trust, nor do they explain what it is to trust.

Robert Solomon and Fernando Flores also take trust to be an emotion, but not a simple feeling, rather, "a profound way of defining our relation to the world."[26] They explain that trustors care both about the outcome and the relationship: "without caring, what is called trust is no more than prediction and reliance."[27] But these conditions, although moving in the right direction, do not distinguish trust from instrumental reliance.

Suppose a police officer Polly has an informant Iris, whom she believes to be truthful. Polly cares about the ongoing relationship—she is concerned for its preservation, hopes it to continue and deepen into the future, and perhaps even daydreams optimistically about the benefits to come, let us say both for her and for her associate. She wants Iris to do well, indeed in the long term, hopes she will take this connection to the non-criminal world as an opportunity to abandon her criminal connections. Yet this is insufficient for trust, not only because it is a contractual relationship with implied, if not actual threats, but also because Polly would replace Iris if a better informant came along. That caring is directed at the relationship as well as outcomes does not make it trustful, resisting the opportunity to renege on the relationship does.[28] An agent can care to preserve an ongoing relationship of reliance.

The point here is not that trust means depending on a particular range of the trusted person's motivations—specifically those motives generated by good will, which is the position defended by Karen Jones—and that trust is misplaced in the absence of such motivations. Rather, an integral part of trust is that the trustor takes herself to be committed, and accepts the appropriate constraints on her conduct. She cares about what she does (not just about the outcome, as Solomon and Flores suggest), and trusting, like trustworthiness, is a kind of fidelity. In cases of mere reliance, or non-trust dependence, there is no such commitment. Trusting involves a special kind of reason for the dependent person to maintain that dependence: she cannot retract it simply because, for instance, a better opportunity becomes available. In cases of mere reliance, the accusation that "you don't trust me" does not gain purchase. When trust, not mere reliance, is at stake, manifest distrust or withdrawal of trust can damage relationships just as untrustworthiness and betrayal can. Commitment explains why some kinds of checking can indicate a lack of trust, and *why* beliefs based on trust are resistant to certain kinds of evidence. This is not to say that judgments to trust are infallible or incorrigible, but that trust generates beliefs that are less amenable to modification than those based on decisions to rely.[29] If I treat a person as one source among others, or accept her word or performance as one of the risks I am prepared to take, that is a case of reliance, not trust. I am committed to those whom I trust, not those on whom I rely, which explains why trust is a form of discrimination between those I trust and those on whom I merely depend, but do not trust.

We can now explain the fourth case of the private investigator example, when a person has evidence that might indicate a partner's infidelity, but is unmoved by it:

4. Right affect absent (replaced by apathy, indifference, distraction, laziness or some other motive) plus temptation to check up, but no distrustful act.

The behavior is superficially the same as in case two, but nothing prevents such an agent from changing her mind and pursuing the option of checking up. She would not be moved by an accusation of distrustful behavior, and does not hold herself to any goal of maintaining the relationship. She might endorse the investigation, for example, for amusement, to encourage her friend's new career path, or for other reasons unconnected with her partner. We can now see that in the first and second cases of possible betrayal, trust was not constituted by the affective attitude, and that the compliant and recalcitrant traits were significant because they enabled (or undermined) the agent's holding to the commitment to trust. Here, both the positive attitude and the commitment to the partner are absent, but in this case there is no trust because there is no commitment.

The importance of affective attitudes is also coming into focus. The affective attitude can motivate the commitment, can ground it securely, and can be a reason for trust. Affective attitudes might be the most common reason for trust, but do not constitute it, since one might make a trustful commitment for reasons of principle, or perhaps duty. Reasons might be combinations of emotions, beliefs, and even habits.

On my account, all failures of trust, whether on the part of the trustor (or one who should trust) or the trusted party are failures of relationship. Failures of trust on behalf of the trusting person are not merely failures to acquire or to convey knowledge, or to cooperate successfully, but are failures to be properly oriented towards other knowers or persons, to be operating properly in the shared environment. I may fail to make the right distinctions between those to trust and those to beware of, or I may fail to recognize when trust is called for, and in each case, I am not exercising the right discriminations and judgments with respect to trust. These failures are the converse of failures to respond appropriately to others' trust. Trust can of course break down when one party behaves untrustworthily, but can also break down when a person fails to trust or withdraws trust inappropriately. Many significant connections *are* constituted by affective attitudes, and trust itself is typically intermeshed with and motivated by emotional connections. But affective attitudes alone don't provide an adequate account of the phenomena because these can be one-sided, and trust is co-constructed.

The emotional attitudes described by Jones and others may typically ac- company, but are not constitutive of, trust. Like trust, betrayal is not redu- cible to an affective response.[30] What is important about betrayal is not its distinctive affect—although a terrible feeling often accompanies a realization of having been betrayed—but whether in fact certain legitimate expectations have been violated. So the identification of a trust context does not depend on subjective feelings of betrayal, but on whether such a response "I trusted you and you betrayed me" would generally be thought appropriate. This is the counterpart to the legitimate accusation "you don't trust me" discussed above.

Two features of the commitment account of trust are important for present purposes. First, the commitment involved in trust is not reducible to any veritistic aim, hence epistemic trust is incompatible with an exclusively veritistic account of epistemic value. It is a commitment, sometimes, precise- ly to forgo some information under conditions of uncertainty, and even when that information could be easily acquired. Thus, ignorance is implicated in trust, even when trust permits knowledge. Second, trust is a non-instrumental relationship between epistemic agents, one in which agents do not treat each other merely as informants. If we were to do so, checking up would never be problematic. Trust illustrates the way that epistemic agents treat one another as agents, not merely as resources for obtaining more knowledge.[31]

The analysis that distinguishes trust and reliance, and shows trust to be a commitment (a virtue of fidelity) has significant advantages over accounts that lack that distinction, since it both explains a certain kind of relationship that arises between epistemic agents, and illuminates a basic structure of the epistemic environment. As potential knowers we do not encounter a flat neutral world of potential informers to be assessed impartially, but one in which some members are taken to be authoritative in some domains. Trust signals that we are prepared to take people as authoritative. At its most fundamental, trust is not a practice that is in need of justification, but is part of the background which shapes and makes possible our epistemic practices, including justification itself.

The connection between trust and ignorance also shows that ignorance is integral to epistemic interdependence. Eliminating ignorance would make trust redundant for an epistemic community. This would be possible only if each of us were able to know all we needed to know independently, that is, without extensive epistemic dependence, or if all dependence were reducible to reliance. But beings like us are not atomistic knowers, nor are we mere instruments, even informing instruments, for one another. We need trust and the relationships that constitute an epistemic community (and therefore an epistemology of trust, community, and ignorance) because our epistemic practices involve us as full epistemic agents who can trust and be trusted, and who can suffer from discredit, as well as exploit gullibility.[32]

Our epistemic environment is necessarily communal. Trust is not a virtue only because our conditions are less than ideal. It is not clear that a collection of independent agents or epistemic instruments *is* superior to an interdependent community, nor is it clear what an appropriate standard of comparison would be because epistemic agents like us, and like Dennis and Christopher discussed in chapter 1 simply are not mere instruments.

Negotiating credibility and authority (both by believing and being believed) are significant parts of epistemic practice, and one who is excluded from trustful interactions cannot exercise the full scope of epistemic agency. Those who are not trusted cannot participate fully in an epistemic community and they always bear an additional burden of showing their dependability where others get credibility for free. Being recognized, acknowledged, and trusted are basic forms of engagement with others as epistemic agents. Without trust, epistemic dependence can only be reliance as if between instruments.[33]

THE GULLIBILITY OBJECTION TO TRUST

Because trust involves a commitment to forgo checking, it inevitably includes ignorance, and being competent with respect to trust is as much about managing ignorance as knowledge. Such differentiated responses are part of what I have learned to do in becoming a member of an epistemic community. My epistemic responsibilities include maintaining my ability to cooperate with others and maintaining the conditions of cooperation, which is not coextensive with maximizing my collection of knowledge or my contribution to others' knowledge collection. But the presence of ignorance is precisely why the "blindness" of trust is sometimes criticized—how can willful ignorance be part of a virtuous epistemic agent's repertoire? Elizabeth Fricker[34] sees proper epistemic dependence as requiring a critical stance, and she argues against accounts of trust similar to the one I defend in that they do not require a hearer to adopt a critical stance with respect to the speaker in order properly to obtain knowledge. Fricker understands the defense of trust as the defense of a stance of always believing unless special circumstances defeat the presumption in favor of belief. While we may obtain knowledge through the testimony of others, Fricker argues that we are not entitled to do so through (uncritical, unreflective) trust, and that we need not do so. That is, she accepts that knowledge can be acquired through testimony, but argues that a hearer is justified in believing the speaker by normal beliefs and evidence about that speaker (which I would term reliance), not by a special epistemic principle concerning trust.

Such a special epistemic principle would, according to Fricker, describe a problematic presumption in favor of believing testimony. "The PR [presumptive right] thesis is an epistemic charter for the gullible and undiscriminating."[35] The key element Fricker identifies in a plausible presumptive right to trust thesis is the "dispensation from the requirement to monitor or assess the speaker for trustworthiness . . . the hearer's critical faculties are not required to be engaged."[36] But when trust is distinguished from reliance, the issue is not merely a dispensation from the monitoring requirement, but an acceptance of the possibility of breaching a relationship by distrust, and a commitment to refrain from doing so. Trust *is* a form of epistemic engagement which can be a basis for knowledge, but it is not explicable as checking and monitoring. Rather, it is inherent in the nature of trust that it enables the bypassing of checking, which makes trust a valuable shortcut to knowledge, and that it requires the neglect of some kinds of pursuit of evidence, which makes ignorance an intrinsic part of trust. There are contexts in which I legitimately acquire knowledge from others, but critical engagement is not the appropriate attitude. I may not have evidence with respect to a speaker, when I engage trustingly with her, but I recognize her as a knower. However, this situation is not the same with respect to every member of the epistemic community with whom I interact. I find myself engaging trustingly with some, and approaching others with a more cautious attitude. Such discriminating responses are best understood as moments of recognition and trusting engagements, not as a tacit inferential process that could in principle be made explicit.[37]

Therefore, a major difference between my account of trust and Fricker's is that she understands trust as indiscriminate because it lacks the risk assessment and checking associated with reliability ascription. She allows for the detection (or recognition) of characteristics that permit the ascription of sincerity and the like to a speaker, but sees this as necessarily governed by critical reflection. That is, she regards critical assessment as the only way that such discriminations could be made, and therefore does not distinguish reliance from trust. But a lack of active critical effort does not equate to gullibility, and gullibility is not the only way to go wrong with respect to epistemic dependence. An epistemic agent needs sometimes to maintain her epistemic relationships by upholding her side of a trustful engagement, and can fail to do so by betrayal or by distrust. Fricker's objection to "gullibility"—that a virtuous epistemic agent should maintain a critical stance—is based on an overly restricted account of the activities and obligations of epistemic agents.

Fricker's view cannot explain some common types of knowledge transactions. Robert Audi offers the example of a chance meeting with someone on a plane who "tells me that, at a conference, a speaker I know lost his temper."[38] Audi suggests that as the conversation develops, I begin "listening in an accepting attitude" and in the end, I come to believe this person, although initially I suspended belief about the temperamental outburst. My relationship with this informant has come to be characterized by trust; I am disposed to believe her. This cannot be as a result of independent evidence about her, as our interaction is confined to a context where I cannot refer to outside information. A relationship of trust has developed and I would suggest that my belief is based on trust not only if I do not anticipate contrary evidence, but because I am neither disposed to seek it nor to be moved by such evidence should it be presented. Up to a point, although not irreversibly, I will stand by my belief in what a trusted person has told me.

Although trustfulness and trustworthiness are characteristics displayed by a virtuous epistemic agent their practice is not good in all circumstances—trust can be misguided, and so can a response of trustworthiness. A virtuous epistemic agent will cultivate and exercise such traits judiciously, not being too hasty to check up whenever it would be easy to acquire further information, because this would undermine relationships of trust, but not being too gullible where checking is appropriate. Such an agent will avoid vicious gullibility and some kinds of vice related to distrust. In some contexts, disbelief, discredit, and suspicion will undermine epistemic relationships, because other knowers are treated with disrespect.[39]

When knowledge is transferred between persons, both the speaker and hearer may need to trust. I may have to trust you to respect and acknowledge what I say before sharing information, and unless you trust what I say, you may be unable to acquire knowledge from me. Unless I trust that you will acknowledge me, and take what I say seriously, I may not even attempt to tell you what I know. Thus, the success of a trustful interaction can depend on the parties' reciprocal recognition and treatment of one another as cooperative epistemic agents.[40]

"Trust" at least sometimes refers to more than predictability. Sometimes I just accept information from a person who offers it. If my friend tells me she was at work late last night, I take it that I know that she was.[41] I do not seek to confirm this fact, and if I did, it would (potentially) indicate a lack of trust.[42] If I treat a person as nothing more than one source among others, that is a case of reliance, not trust. Reliance can be reduced to risk-assessment and judgment of probabilities, but trust concerns the connections between epistemic agents. This is not to say that evidence is never relevant to trust, but that trust cannot be reduced to critical judgment and evaluation of evidence. Simple evidentialism[43] cannot encompass responsible trust.

Denying that trust is primarily based in evidence invites the following objection. Something must form the basis for my trust, and in a sense this must be evidence, because all my experience and observation can be classed as "evidence." However, there is a difference between taking my observations as evidence and (explicitly or tacitly) making use of them in a process of inference, and directly accepting what a speaker tells me by simply believing her. I construe these as different ways of engaging with a speaker, different ways of responding to the person who conveys information. I may treat her words as evidence, and treat her as a source like any other, which I term reliance. If I engage with her as a trusted person, I recognize and acknowledge her as a knower, and am committed to some extent to believing her. It probably must be the case that some of my past experience or observations motivate my trustful engagements, but this is not the same as dealing with the person as I would deal with evidence. In fact, I may select a source of information with trust in mind. I choose my medical practitioner assuming a standard level of competence and expertise common to many practitioners, and I presume that I can depend on the information she gives me. Among my selection criteria is the desire to deal with someone with whom I can engage properly, whom I can trust and respect, and who will trust and respect me. The potential for trust is a proper consideration for a relationship in which the exchange of information will be important.

ELICITING TRUST

We are sometimes obliged to trust, just as we are sometimes obliged to be trustworthy[44] and this means ignorance is intrinsic to some epistemic obligations. An account of trust needs to explain how there can be an obligation to trust and how trust can elicit trustworthy responses from a trusted person. The account of trust as a commitment can explain that trust involves reciprocal obligations. When I trust, I am not only at risk in some way if my trust is misplaced, I am restricted in what I can do compatibly with trusting. I make or find myself with a commitment to thinking well of that person, and acting and interpreting evidence in accord with this commitment. I cannot trust and simultaneously protect myself against the possibility that I might be let down, but my reliance can incorporate a great deal of doubt about motive, success, or competence and protection against unreliability. And just because others have an optimistic attitude towards me, or confident expectations about my behavior, it need not be the case that they trust me, nor that I am called upon to respond to that positive attitude. It is the commitment of a trusting person that calls forth the response from a trustee.

Trust calls for and encourages a response of trustworthiness. Philip Pettit offers an interpretation of this phenomenon.[45] He describes one motivation for trustworthy responsiveness as the "relatively base desire to be well considered."[46] With respect to epistemic trust, however, it is not merely a desire to be well thought of that elicits trustworthy responses: unless one is trusted and acknowledged, one cannot be a full participant in epistemic interactions. So it is not the case that we are motivated to be dependable merely because manifesting trustworthiness affords opportunities to "savor the good opinion of others."[47] Being recognized as dependable or trustworthy affords opportunities to act as an informant, to be taken seriously when asking for confirmation or justification, to corroborate what others say and so on.

Bernd Lahno's characterization of trust as an emotion leads him to a different error with respect to deliberate trust. He describes a teacher trusting an impulsive student with certain responsibilities in the hope that she will live up to them and comments that "one may feel that the trust is somehow feigned."[48] It is, he suggests, a "manipulation" of the student, in which the "real beliefs" of the teacher must be kept hidden. This assessment is motivated, I think, by Lahno's conviction that if trust is sincere, it must involve genuine emotion. "The teacher is lacking the attitude necessary for the sort of trust he is signaling."[49] So it turns out that absent such an appropriate emotional attitude, there is no trust. A person without these attitudes who manifests trust is to some extent "concealing his real beliefs and motivation."[50] But this is too quick. We encounter opportunities for trust in very complex circumstances, with more or less insight into our own psyches, cultures, prejudices, and emotional states. These elements are not always, if ever, fully transparent and some of these aspects may conflict. It is not at all clear that there is one pattern of "real beliefs" or one clearly differentiated emotional attitude or set of attitudes that an agent or observer can identify. Instead, we may see the teacher's situation as one that might approximate fully-fledged trust more or less closely. The teacher could manifest trustful behavior manipulatively (even dishonestly) as Lahno proposes, but a deliberate signal of trust need not be like that. Even if the teacher is motivated by a desire to inspire responsibility in the impulsive student, she may be committing herself by this trustful action, and if so, on my account, this is genuine trust. The teacher can consciously reform her thoughts and actions to align with the constraints and obligations of a trusting relationship, which is to say that she commits herself and comes to trust. In fact, we know that trust can be cultivated, and as Jones points out, various circumstances can motivate a desire to learn to trust. A realization that I have internalized a cultural suspicion of people of certain race, gender, sexuality, class or ethno-cultural affiliation, or an experience that damages my trust can prompt deliberate efforts to trust more wisely (more widely, more narrowly, or with a different configuration). Indeed, understanding trust as a commitment allows a more subtle understanding of deliberate entry into trust-like relationships than is available from the attitudinal accounts.[51] Lahno would use emotion to distinguish genuine trust from fake or pretended trust used to manipulate or exploit others. On my account, cases of deceit and fraud via manipulation or exploitation are not real trust because there is no commitment on the part of the trustor, and the engagement places no constraint on her future (or present) behavior. The analysis of Lahno's own example suggests that an emotional character is not an essential ingredient of trust.

Trust can be dangerous. The alignment of trust and gullibility is not entirely wrongheaded; trust can make us vulnerable to exploitation as well as error. That trust is indispensable does not mean that in every instance it is wise or advantageous, but that it is part of the repertoire of a competent epistemic agent, and, as discussed, it can be mis-oriented. As Edward Craig points out, managing to identify good informants is an essential (he thinks definitive) part of epistemic practice.[52]

Precisely because the discrimination involved in trust is not merely a *belief* about a person's report or judgment of her character, nor an attitude of optimism or confident expectation, trust and distrust can significantly affect those who are trusted or those from whom trust is withheld. Trust is a way of relating to persons as agents or knowers in their own right, as Lahno correctly acknowledges when he calls trust a participant attitude.[53] (But note that many interactions require such an attitude including threats and manipulations.) As Jones suggests, trust involves "the expectation that the one trusted will be directly and favorably moved by the thought that we are counting on her."[54] The fact that trust can have this kind of effect can be a reason to cultivate trust, as it is for the teacher in the above example. Jones claims that trust is self-confirming as I will both notice and elicit responses that affirm my optimistic attitude. But, for Jones and other attitudinists, the question remains: *How* does trust have the power to call forth such a response? It cannot be the mere taking of a risk, nor just a positive expectation—nothing obliges me to act in accord with your optimism. Charity collectors know this only too well. The trusting person is committed to believing the person she trusts, not to double-checking and the trusted person responds to this *commitment*. Trust builds connections between persons and at its most fundamental, trust is the background which shapes and makes possible our practices of dependence and which orients us to evidence.

The attitudinal accounts of trust correctly identify positive expectations and emotions that tend to accompany trust. But these features are accidental, and what is essential about trust is that it is a mode of engagement between agents that, like promising, is a form of fidelity. Trust shapes my view of the trusting context by constraining my interpretations of evidence and it also shapes my possible beliefs and behavior: how I can act with respect to the trust context. These limits are, of course, revisable—trust can be revoked—but I am nevertheless committed to them, to the extent, and for the duration of my trust. Trust involves an engagement and a commitment, not just an assessment of risk, or a judgment of justification or warrant. Trusting well is not reducible to believing those who know best or most, and the avoidance of being misled. It is about maintaining epistemic respect and avoiding epistemic insult, such as discredit in the modes of disbelief, distrust, and refusal to acknowledge.

Maintaining trust sometimes requires retaining ignorance. I do not monitor the reliableness of another knower: if I did, I would show that trust was lacking. I could not claim that my seeking evidence of the person's reliability was intended to strengthen my trust—trust does not work like that. Cases where I am trying to establish or cultivate trust are different, because these are like trying to overturn *distrust*. For example, if I say "I will trust you just this once" I am pointing to my distrust.

So trust is not just a summary of direct or background evidence. It shapes how evidence appears to me, and what I can look for, and insofar as this is restricted by trust, ignorance is ineliminable. Trust often mandates privacy, confidentiality, and non-pursuit of potential knowledge—in a word, ignorance. Trust allows the replacement of ignorance with knowledge, but in doing so, it mandates that other areas of ignorance remain undisturbed. All epistemic dependence offers valuable epistemic shortcuts and access to otherwise unavailable knowledge, and in this sense, trust enables the acquisition of knowledge, but the functions of trust differ from the functions of reliance. Reliance allows me to ask for and obtain information, and trust overlaps to some extent. Trust also is needed for the way we depend on others to develop, maintain, and modify judgments about evidence or justification and other epistemic competences. If I am uncertain about my competence in a certain domain, I need trustworthy others to ask for feedback. This is trust not for information, but for orienting my own self-trust. I need to trust others to establish and to ensure my own trustworthiness and epistemic authority.

David Hume refers to the importance of recognition when he states:

> There is no algebraist or Mathematician so expert in his science, as to place entire confidence in any truth immediately upon his discovery of it, or regard it as any thing, but a mere probability. Every time he runs over his proofs, his confidence encreases; but still more by the approbation of his friends; and is rais'd to its utmost perfection by the universal assent and applauses of the learned world.[55]

The importance of credibility and acknowledgment goes beyond a simple desire to convey truth; they locate agents in authoritative positions with respect to others in the epistemic community. The acknowledgment of others in the epistemic community makes a difference to the mathematician as an epistemic agent whose concerns are not just those of increasing knowledge and information. In order to conduct oneself in a range of epistemic interactions—to cooperate, learn, teach, testify, and so on—it is necessary that one is thought well of as a knower by one's epistemic peers.

PROBLEMATIC TRUST

Trust can be granted or withheld for reasons other than trustworthiness, and reasons based on identity stereotypes are particularly pernicious. Lahno's reservations about deliberate trust are partly based on this feature of epistemic relationships. Lessons from Braaten's analysis, discussed in chapter 1, of the intellectual virtues aimed at reflection on the kind of community we have and the kind of community we might want can reveal how social patterns of credibility come apart from trustworthiness. Kristina Rolin argues that a normatively adequate account of testimony must address not just the extent of epistemic dependence, but also the role of communities in guaranteeing trustworthiness, and the possibility of divergence between credibility and trustworthiness, especially for members of non-privileged social groups.[56] Rolin argues that, alongside other forms of exclusion, combative styles of interaction in some scientific communities "can make it harder for women scientists to fully participate in academic conversation."[57] Rolin proposes instead that "There have to be norms of civility that guarantee that all members of the community are entitled to be heard and to be responded to respectfully"[58] in order to ensure inclusive and responsive dialogue which can make sure that all ideas and criticisms can contribute to scientific development.

These "norms of civility" are part of epistemic practice, and reflection on the community's norms are part of epistemic responsibility. These norms and the effects of upholding or disregarding them are significant not only because exclusions might lead to sub-optimal (perhaps biased) research projects, but also because full exercise of epistemic agency is a good for us, and inhibition, exclusion, and discredit are bad for us. These valuable aspects of epistemic life are not reducible to amounts of knowledge acquired or shared.

But care is needed to avoid presuming that only one mode of interacting is available or appropriate, when we consider ways of establishing or demonstrating trustworthiness. Patricia Williams contrasts her approach to "bargaining relations" (specifically house-renting) with that of a colleague:

> It turned out that Peter had handed over a $900 deposit in cash, with no lease, no exchange of keys, and no receipt to strangers with whom he had no ties other than a few moments of pleasant conversation. . . . In my rush to show

good faith and trustworthiness, I signed a detailed, lengthily negotiated, finely printed lease firmly establishing me as the ideal arms-length transactor.[59]

Since both renters are lawyers, the difference in approach is not based in the presence or absence of professional familiarity with contractual negotiations. Rather, Williams suggests that it is a difference in the need for a black woman to establish trustworthiness, while in contrast, as a white man, her colleague finds, as he expects, that his trustworthiness can be taken for granted. In many contexts, those who have to work harder to establish their authority or credentials, or whose authority and credentials are denied are disadvantaged, facing an extra cost in, or exclusion from certain transactions.[60] Williams shows her trustworthiness by presenting her preparedness to make an explicit commitment—she won't be the first to breach it. But she faces a (perceived or actual) demand that she demonstrate this—and this demand indicates that trust is not (yet) present. Her colleague can take for granted that he will be perceived as trustworthy.

On my analysis of the difference between reliance and trust, the provision of a contract can establish reliability, so can motivate reliance, but need not motivate trust. If Williams provided references to her prospective landlord, it would seem *prima facie* compatible with the relationship so far that she or he might check them. It would seem less clear that Peter's new landlord could check up on the informal information he provided, for example about where he worked, during their "pleasant conversation," without disrupting the relationship established so far. For those of us privileged enough to take our credibility for granted, it is possible to forget that this is not universal. Certainly, a theory about epistemic interdependence is flawed if it fails to recognize this aspect of epistemic life.[61] To be authoritative, trustworthy, and responsible are goods for an epistemic agent, but mere possession of these virtues is not sufficient for their exercise by a knower in community. She, like Hume's mathematician, and like Patricia Williams, needs further that her fellows recognize and acknowledge these attributes, that she is accredited and granted credence. Both trustfulness and trustworthiness are characteristic of a virtuous epistemic agent who will cultivate such traits and exercise them judiciously. Furthermore, virtuous agents will avoid some kinds of vice related to distrust. In some contexts, disbelief, discredit, and suspicion will undermine epistemic relationships, because other knowers are treated with disrespect.

CASSANDRA AND THE NON-VERITISTIC VALUE OF TRUST

The story of Cassandra, a mythical character who was cursed by Apollo so that no one would believe her true prophecies, underlines the importance of acknowledgment.[62] I will derive the following argument from the story:

1. Cassandra incurs epistemic damage when she is cursed by Apollo;
2. Cassandra has not lost knowledge or the capacity to know;
3. The curse has damaged another dimension (or dimensions) of Cassandra's epistemic agency.

Apollo tries to seduce Cassandra by bribing her with the gift of prophecy. When she refuses him, she is punished by having her credibility taken away. Her words gain no credence—no one will believe her. Apollo does not merely return Cassandra to her pre-prophetic state—that is, to the state of a normal knower. Despite allowing her to keep the gift of prophecy, a *prima facie* enhancement of her epistemic status, he takes credibility away from her; he damages her by declaring her untrustworthy.[63] To be disbelieved and distrusted is a curse. And importantly, this curse is directed at her—not at any others who might suffer from being deprived of her knowledge. Though arguably his act does have such effects, Apollo is not aiming to punish or benefit others through Cassandra.

Cassandra does not lack information or knowledge.[64] What Cassandra loses when she is cursed is the capacity to participate in epistemic relationships that require acknowledgment and reciprocity, those things essential to epistemic agents understood as mutually dependent members of an epistemic community. Cassandra cannot defend her claims to know and she has no discretion with respect to disclosure—she cannot choose to reveal or conceal what she knows. Everything she knows and claims is tarred with the same brush and will receive the same incredulous response. She cannot select what to communicate, nor can she determine the extent of what she shares. Because she cannot entrust another with what she knows, Cassandra is excluded from cooperative interactions. She cannot demonstrate her trust in another by confiding a secret—she cannot exercise or manifest judgment about the modes of her interactions with other knowers. Precisely because she is excluded from these kinds of interaction, Cassandra cannot practice certain kinds of intellectual virtues. These are explored in chapter 1's discussion of the interplay between Dennis and Christopher, and are described by Lorraine Code in this way: "Intellectual goodness, consists, then, in conducting one's moral and intellectual life so as to contribute to the creation and preservation of the best possible standards appropriate to the practices within which one lives."[65] Cassandra cannot manifest or partake in these goods because the curse fully excludes her from her epistemic community. Cases where participation is limited by stereotype or prejudice are familiar not only from fiction, but from many people's lives. People who are treated with disbelief like Cassandra suffer an injustice of a distinctly epistemic kind, in addition to other direct and indirect costs of being a victim of injustice.

In describing mechanisms of the interdependence of actual epistemic agents, it becomes increasingly clear that increasing knowledge with the aim of eliminating ignorance cannot account for the range of virtues and values that matter to us. Trust is an epistemic practice that cannot be reduced to maximizing or optimizing the exchange of information, a practice in which all we need do is calculate the risks, costs, and benefits of depending on other agents. Without recognizing the distinction between forms of epistemic dependence, common epistemic practices cannot be well explained. Without acknowledging the role of ignorance, an account of trust will be distorted, inadequate, or absent. Ignorance is embedded in the structure of trust, and unless this is incorporated in the analysis, trust is either conflated with, or dismissed because it is not, risk assessment. As shown, one distinctively epistemic component (forgoing checking) is left out, as in the affective accounts. From the side of epistemology, it is an excessive love of knowledge that distorts the understanding of trust—it is seen only as a means of acquiring knowledge and judged in those terms. Either trust is akin to gullibility and rejected, or it is a good strategy that can be justified and accepted. It is either a good way to eliminate ignorance, or not. The above discussion shows how trust differs from reliance and how the distinctive character of trust involves ineliminable ignorance. Trust and reliance are both important forms of epistemic dependence. Showing how they are distinct shows that epistemic agents need to do more than assist others' collection of information, and how the scope of epistemic virtue extends beyond mere reliability.

The importance of credibility and trust means that status and authority are epistemic concerns, as well as being matters of ethical and political significance. The division of epistemic labor organizes institutional arrangements of epistemic authority as well as practices of discovery and access to information. In the next chapter, this understanding will be applied to institutionalized epistemic practices. Here, too, ignorance is integral to a range of practices and to a successful analysis of institutional epistemic dependence.

Epistemic agents evaluate others' credibility based on comportment, stereotypes, and appearance, as well as on the reasons they articulate. Likewise, as testifiers, we have more or less deliberate embodied styles of comportment that either enhance or undermine our credibility relative to more or less explicit standards. The possibility of epistemic injustice arises because stereotypes and relationships of oppression, domination, subordination, and the like can affect how epistemic agents accord credence differentially to members of diverse social groups. It is culturally easy for me to treat as authoritative a person with familiar marks of authority, for example a male, white, able-bodied figure, with appropriate trappings of professional status. Less easy is recognizing as authoritative figures whose bodily appearance and capacity, accent, class, and the like depart from this stereotype. Credibility is always social, so questions of epistemic welfare must go beyond knowledge collection to these social group questions and must intersect with questions of justice.

As Rae Langton has pointed out in a review of Miranda Fricker's *Epistemic Injustice*, structural changes will be needed to address epistemic injustice.[66] It isn't enough for individual epistemic agents to adopt more virtuous practices—we cannot simply identify, then eradicate or compensate for our implicit biases. It is more effective in many contexts to adopt a structure that disables such biases, as anonymous evaluation systems can often do. And such adoptions need to be widespread, systematic. A community can hence become more virtuous even if its individual members don't change much.

EPISTEMICALLY RESPONSIBLE TRUST

Concern for credibility and attention to the power of stereotypes to drive a wedge between perceived and actual trustworthiness are increasingly important topics within social epistemology. Feminist epistemologists are particularly interested in how gender affects epistemic status, and how epistemic agents might do better in this area. Miranda Fricker's conception of the (epistemic) virtue of reflexive critical openness[67] is an example of a virtue valuable not only because it may contribute to knowledge, but also because it enhances epistemic justice. It is a stance toward others that is open to their being authoritative testifiers, but reflexively critical, so that a hearer of testimony can check that their own attitude towards another's credibility is well founded. Fricker shows that one group may be prejudiced against another's social credibility, and suggests that one may, by carefully attending to the power relations between the parties, correct for certain prejudices and the testimonial injustices they tend to encourage. Like Fricker, I argue that there are epistemic motivations to avoid testimonial injustice, not only because hearers lose opportunities to gain knowledge, but also because being disbelieved can be an epistemic loss to a potential testifier. An agent can suffer epistemic loss because others fail to recognize her as a knower.

These harms and virtues are matters of both individual and collective responsibility. An individual hearer can manifest a corrective virtue to mitigate identity prejudice, but more is needed. A culture or community can have structures that perpetuate entrenched prejudices and patterns of credence that overwhelm individual efforts, and there can be other structures (such as anonymizing) that will work better than self-correction to mitigate those patterns. Virtues of epistemic justice can be directed at one's own conduct, at promoting virtuous dispositions in other agents and at establishing systems conducive to epistemic justice that do not depend on individual intentions or efforts to be maintained. Hence it is crucial to consider collective and structural arrangements as well as considering what epistemic agents can do to be more virtuous.

Fricker presents the example of Marge Sherwood from Anthony Minghella's screenplay of *The Talented Mr. Ripley*. Marge suffers epistemic discredit as she is disbelieved. She knows that Tom Ripley has killed her fiancé Dickie Greenleaf, but, prompted by Ripley, Greenleaf senior and the private detective Macarron patronizingly dismiss her concern as hysterical. Fricker plausibly suggests that if Dickie's mother had been there, her attitude to Marge's testimony might well have been different, exemplifying how the interaction between social group memberships can affect credibility and uptake. (It isn't clear how Macarron might have responded to Mrs. Greenleaf—perhaps her belief in Marge would have persuaded him to take her views more seriously, or perhaps she, too, would have been dismissed.) In Fricker's words "the result is a collusion of men against Marge's word being taken seriously."[68] This suggests that Mrs. Greenleaf would, like Marge Sherwood, be on the wrong side of a gendered credibility pattern.

A counterfactual variation on Fricker's case shows the limitations of an epistemic assessment based only on achievement of knowledge. Suppose immediately after Marge Sherwood leaves the scene, Mr. Macarron and Mr. Greenleaf were to receive testimony with the same content as that Marge offered, from a person who they are disposed to take seriously. Perhaps it is another male investigator, whose insight cannot be put down to "female intuition." The deficit in Greenleaf's and Macarron's knowledge is remedied, with minimal delay, so from an epistemophiliac point of view that knowledge is all that counts, all is well. It would not really matter who the source actually was since in both cases, everyone now knows the relevant information.[69] But I want to say, as Fricker suggests, that in their treatment of Marge Sherwood, Mr. Greenleaf and Mr. Macarron do not do well as members of an epistemic community, and that this defect is not fully accounted for by their failure to acquire knowledge on this occasion. Thus the credibility defect is an epistemic harm to Marge and an epistemic vice (whether or not culpable) on the side of those who do not or cannot see her as believable. An epistemic community in which such attitudes prevail is thereby impoverished and damaging to its members. One corrective virtue is a critical awareness, that can be self-directed, and which manifested by a hearer could mitigate identity prejudice. But more is needed—a culture and community whose structures discourage and counteract the patterns of credence and mis-credence associated with entrenched prejudices. Where invested ignorance is manifest, it obstructs agents' self-identification as succumbing to mis-credence and the like, and so such patterns are better addressed through systemic change, rather than individual effort.

The point is not that an epistemophiliac who loves knowledge would endorse the kind of systematic illegitimate discredit experienced by those who lack social privilege—of course not. An epistemophiliac would point out that our interest is in veritism, believing truths, and thus we have an interest in having our habits of credence track who is telling the truth, not some prejudice or stereotype.[70] Manifesting a reliable disposition to avoid such prejudice is simply part of good knowledge acquisition practice. Even if, as in the revised case above, the error from failure to accept testimony is remedied without delay, the epistemophiliac can still reject the attitude. However the epistemophiliac does so only for its disutility, because it fails to conduce to the goal of believing the optimal proportion of truths over false-hoods. This account of epistemic value does not show and cannot show that a speaker who is unjustly disbelieved suffers an epistemic loss. I argue that there is such a loss, that it is distinctly epistemic, and that the epistemophilic value is inadequate to account for such a loss.

If the only epistemic values were those concerning the acquisition and dissemination of facts, evidence, and information, Cassandra's loss would be unintelligible as an epistemic harm, but those values do not tell the whole story. The importance of recognition and credibility are left out of accounts that pay insufficient attention to the shared epistemic environment. This loss cannot be characterized as failure to achieve a veritistic outcome, since Cassandra and Marge Sherwood have knowledge, the problem is their inability to share it, a lack of uptake. The scope and range of their epistemic interactions is restricted, in a way that is properly termed epistemic injustice or subordination or oppression. Nor is mere failure to acquire knowledge the whole story of the failures of Macarron and Ripley senior—they also fail to live up to the virtue of epistemic justice. These examples show that it is not only our capacities to deal with facts and evidence that are epistemically valuable, but also our engagements with other agents as participants in an epistemic community. A complete account of epistemic values must include an account of those related to how knowers interact, and how the community is structured, not just those related to the acquisition of justified beliefs, truth, and empirical evidence.

Miranda Fricker states in an earlier discussion: "I take it that basic forms of epistemic agency, such as functioning as an informant on everyday matters, is indeed one of the essential attributes of person hood—it is part and parcel of being accepted as a compatriot in the community of the rational. If this is so, then an epistemic climate in which some people suffer systematic testimonial injustice must be regarded as seriously defective, both epistemically and ethically."[71] The upshot of this discussion is that epistemic agents and their epistemic community may be evaluated not just according to who knows what (recall the earlier discussion about assessing a community's knowledge), but according to whether the agent displays or the community encourages the kind of epistemic justice Fricker identifies, and the kinds of imaginative and evaluative virtue that Braaten presents in thinking about the nature of one's community.[72] The conditions for individuals to possess such social virtues are not just a matter of individual responsibility, but are partially constituted by the invisible networks of expectation, stereotype, epistemic privilege, and authority that pervade epistemic communities, like diffuse Foucauldian power. These background social conditions (partially) constitute our identities as epistemic agents, as well as telling us who to believe, what are the markers of authority, and the like. Persons have epistemic authority not just because they have more knowledge, but because they are in recognized authoritative positions with respect to knowledge. These conditions can encourage us to remain complacent in our prejudices and thus allow epistemic injustices to continue unchecked, or can support the virtue Fricker describes. It is part of the role of epistemologists to identify and explicate such social epistemic virtues; both those that can be adopted by individuals, and those that can make a community more just, even if individuals don't all change (and sometimes we cannot).

Fricker argues that the failure to believe testimony because of prejudice might be more or less culpable, depending on whether the agent has a sound deliberative route to forming such a belief, perhaps via critical reflection on his or her own prejudices. In some social-historical circumstances, the insights and critical concepts necessary for such reflection might not be available. Then, the agent's failure to achieve veritistic results by appropriate uptake of testimony is unfortunate, but not blameworthy. This is a plausible view of the potential believer of testimony's responsibility. It also reinforces the responsibility of those whose role it is to analyse epistemic virtues to pay attention such attitudes, and to make them available for consideration. But the whole story, I have argued, is not reducible to failure to achieve veritistic results.

The capacity to reflect on how we deal with others' testimony is an important virtue, related to those proposed by Braaten (discussed in chapter 1) that contribute to how we make our community work. We might be more or less oblivious to habitual patterns of perceiving or stereotyping others, we might be more or less sensitized to differences that can affect our assessment of others' credibility. Looking others in the eye in dominant Anglo Australian society is a way of signaling that one is direct, straightforward and honest, but for members of other cultures, including some indigenous Australian communities, such a direct gaze is disrespectful, and one should keep one's eyes lowered in front of figures of authority and seniority. So a signal of respect might be construed as a sign of shiftiness, or a signal of honesty as a sign of disrespect, if members of such groups interact and these different styles are unarticulated and unavailable for critical reflection. It is important to be aware of shared tendencies that might contribute to unjust incredulity, and maintaining this awareness, and implementing structural protections against patterns of injustice are part of epistemic practice.

It seems likely that anti-prejudicial virtues are often truth-conducive, but their value does not reside exclusively in this veritistic utility. Their value also rests in their contribution to the relationships that constitute a healthy and sustainable epistemic community. Not only do these relationships involve ignorance as well as knowledge, they are not fostered by an exclusive focus on eliminating ignorance.

Common to Fricker's and Rolin's discussions is a concern for how epistemic agents are treated, Fricker in informal cases of epistemic injustice, Rolin within scientific practice. This can have instrumental value as contributing to veritistic increase, but I have argued that the value of treating epistemic agents as such goes beyond its veritistic import. The reasons for cultivating the conditions for trust, credibility, and authority are that these are constitutive parts of epistemic agency, valuable in their own right, not reducible to veritistic outcomes, and not to be substituted even if equally good veritistic outcomes were available.

NOTES

1. See, for example, Londa Schiebinger, *Plants and Empire: Colonial Bioprospecting in the Atlantic World* (Cambridge, MA: Harvard University Press, 2004); Nancy Tuana, "The Speculum of Ignorance: The Women's Health Movement and Epistemologies of Ignorance," *Hypatia* 21, no. 3 (2006): 1–19.

2. Goldman, "Epistemic Paternalism," 113–31.

3. Miranda Fricker, "Epistemic Injustice and a Role for Virtue in the Politics of Knowing," *Metaphilosophy* 34, no. 1/2 (2003): 172.

4. Goldman sees this as recognized in epistemically paternalistic rules for legally admissible evidence and policies for news providers. Goldman, "Epistemic Paternalism," 113–31.

5. A distinction between "trust" and "reliance" is not consistently maintained in ordinary language or epistemology: it is possible to discuss trust without drawing a distinction between it and reliance, but rather making one a part of the other. For example, Philip Pettit sees trust as a form of reliance. Philip Pettit, "The Cunning of Trust," *Philosophy and Public Affairs* 24, no. 3 (1995): 202–225. Lawrence Becker conversely defines three forms of trust: credulity, or "a disposition to believe what another person says and to banish skeptical thoughts;" reliance, or "a disposition to depend upon other people in some respect;" and security, or "a disposition to have confidence about other people's motives, to banish suspicious thoughts about them." Lawrence C. Becker, "Trust as Noncognitive Security about Motives," *Ethics* 107 (1996): 45–6. On his account, these forms of trust can be independent. That is, according to Becker, I can believe without feeling secure about a person's motives, or depending on them in any obvious way. Conversely, I can depend on someone without understanding what they say, so I am not in a position to believe. Each of these is a form of trust. However, rather than identifying credulity, reliance, and security as different kinds of trust, I think it is better to retain a distinction between trust and reliance, without presupposing that all epistemic trust is about

beliefs. It seems plausible that we do rely without trusting, and even vice versa, and that trust involves different forms of engagement than reliance, or just belief. This is reflected in the powerful normative connotations of terms like "trust" and "trustworthy." Becker's account extends "trust" to include any case of dependence. I use "dependence" as the umbrella term that encompasses forms of trust and reliance because there are distinct literatures dealing with reliabilism and trust and they have been discussed separately in relation to testimony, the acquisition of knowledge from another's say-so. I am not insisting that together these exhaust the range of epistemic dependencies; they probably do not, but the distinction I am drawing is important whichever terms are used to describe it.

6. Doing so is important because, among other things, such authority can be treated as transitive. If my historian colleague tells me that the author of a new history book is a good historian, I can treat the book's contents as authoritative. More generally, specialists can know who is good in their own and related fields, and non-specialists can recognize good authorities by their status in the relevant disciplines. I return to the division of epistemic labor in the following chapter.

7. J. E. Adler, "Testimony, Trust, Knowing," *The Journal of Philosophy* 91, no. 5 (1994): 264–75; Goldman, 1999.

8. A crucial difference is that an epistemic agent is a person, and as such, unique and irreplaceable in a way that a mere instrument is not.

9. For some discussion of the complex dimensions of trust and being trustworthy, see Nancy Nyquist Potter, *How Can I Be Trusted?: A Virtue Theory of Trustworthiness* (Maryland: Rowman and Littlefield, 2002).

10. Invested ignorance is important for the way that trust and credibility are distributed, but it is a kind of ignorance that should be challenged or contested, and here I am interested in ignorance that is not eliminable.

11. I am indebted to discussions with Justine McGill and to an anonymous reviewer for Lexington Books for pushing me to greater clarity on these issues.

12. Compare chapter 1's discussion of Hall and Johnson, "The Epistemic Duty."

13. Jack Meiland, "What Ought We To Believe? or the Ethics of Belief Revisited," *American Philosophical Quarterly* 17 (1980): 16.

14. The classical case is supposed to be infidelity, but many other interpretations such as the husband's being a cross-dresser with the wig-maker's phone number are possible. (Thanks to Mitch Parsell for this point.)

15. Here, notice that a degree of trust is required for the initial request (or demand) for an explanation. Conceivably in some cases, there might be insufficient trust in a relationship to think it could survive such a conversation (or confrontation). The example is intended to be neutral on the wisdom or justifiedness of her trusting him. The point is to define the character of trust, not to defend or condemn trust in this instance.

16. Take this to include all of the conditions discussed below including patterns of attention and tendencies of interpretation.

17. I thank a Lexington Books reviewer for clarifying this point.

18. Bernd Lahno, "On the Emotional Character of Trust," *Ethical Theory and Moral Practice* 4 (2001): 171–89; Karen Jones, "Trust as an Affective Attitude," *Ethics* 107 (1996): 4–25.

19. See for example Robert Hardin, "Trustworthiness," *Ethics* 107 (1996): 26–42. A somewhat different perspective is presented by Elizabeth Fricker, who equates trust with gullibility, or foolishness, or failure with respect to risk assessment. Elizabeth Fricker, "The Epistemology of Testimony," *The Aristotelian Society, Supplementary Volume* 61 (1987): 57–84.

20. Jones, "Trust as an Affective Attitude," 4.

21. Lahno, "Emotional Character of Trust," 175.

22. Lahno, "Emotional Character of Trust," 182.

23. Lahno, "Emotional Character of Trust," 180.

24. Lahno acknowledges De Sousa and Calhoun as sources for the theory of emotions on which he relies. See Ronald de Sousa, *The Rationality of Emotion* (Cambridge, MA: MIT Press, 1987); Cheshire Calhoun, "Cognitive Emotions?," in *What is an Emotion? Classical Readings in Philosophical Psychology*, ed. C. Calhoun and R. C. Solomon (New York and Oxford: Oxford University Press, 1984).

25. Jones, "Trust as an Affective Attitude," 20.

26. Robert C. Solomon and Fernando Flores, *Building Trust: In Business, Politics, Relationships, and Life* (Oxford: Oxford University Press, 2003), 104–5.

27. Solomon and Flores, *Building Trust*, 105.

28. Caring understood as ongoing preservation complicates this point because it is ambiguous between the kind of commitment I have in mind, and a motivation to preserve the relationship because of calculated benefit that could be replaced.

29. This is one of the phenomena Jones sees as in need of explanation. Jones, "Trust as an Affective Attitude," 15.

30. Recognition of unfairness is often accompanied by resentment, but need not be: I may lack completely the relevant distinctive and affectively loaded way of seeing the situation, even if I concede that it was unfair. Conversely, resentment does not explain that I have been treated unfairly.

31. This posits a stronger kind of epistemic agency than Craig's informant/source distinction.

32. For extensive and rich discussion of the importance of epistemic agency and the profound implications of its being damaged, see Miranda Fricker, *Epistemic Injustice.*

33. I argue for the importance of trust and credibility in Cynthia Townley, "Trust and the Curse of Cassandra," *Philosophy in the Contemporary World* 10, no. 2 (2003): 105–12. See also Nancy Nyquist Potter's discussion of uptake in Potter, *How Can I be Trusted?*, 147–80.

34. Fricker, "Against Gullibility," in *Knowing From Words*, ed. B. K. Matilal and A. Chakrabarti (Dordrecht: Kluwer, 1994).

35. Fricker, "Against Gullibility," 126.

36. Fricker, "Against Gullibility," 144.

37. These discriminations need not be benign; for example, they can problematically track pernicious stereotypes.

38. Robert Audi, "The Place of Testimony in the Fabric of Knowledge and Justification," *American Philosophical Quarterly* 34, no. 4 (1997): 407.

39. In a paper titled "Other Minds," Austin notices this feature of epistemic relationships. He points out "[i]f I have said I know or I promise, you insult me in a special way by refusing to accept it." J. L. Austin, "Other Minds" in *J. L. Austin: Philosophical Papers*, 2nd ed, ed. J. O. Urmson and G. J. Warnock (Oxford: Clarendon Press, 1970), 100.

40. The need to be trusted in order to participate and to share social protections is not always clear to those who have the privilege of being trusted. For example, members of some social groups, or victims of some kinds of crimes who do not expect to be believed (often with good reason) will be inhibited in reporting to authorities, and can be excluded from formal justice.

41. I have not been to where my sister works, nor has she visited the university campus where I work. But I think she knows quite a lot about it from what I have told her, as I do about her work environment.

42. It is not necessary that I have a history with my informant—I could trust a stranger for directions. But the possibility of spontaneous trust is parasitic on the establishment of competence with respect to trusting, and this will generally arise within relationships of longer duration.

43. See endnote 6.

44. I am not here attempting to offer a full account of when trust is obligatory, although I gesture toward some kinds of cases below, nor am I seeking to offer an account of when trustworthiness is obligatory. My view is that one ought not trust indiscriminately, nor should one necessarily be trustworthy, if, for example, cooperation or complicity in exploitation or injustice is involved.

45. Pettit, "The Cunning of Trust."

46. Pettit, "The Cunning of Trust," 203.

47. Pettit, "The Cunning of Trust," 219.

48. Lahno, "Emotional Character of Trust," 184.

49. Lahno, "Emotional Character of Trust," 184.

50. Lahno, "Emotional Character of Trust," 185.

51. To the extent that my account of the teacher-student interaction is plausible, and clearly Lahno's and my intuitions diverge on this point, it suggests that emotional character is not necessary for trust. Notice, moreover, that these descriptions of withdrawal, absence, and cultivation of trust are framed without reference to emotions, affect or feelings.

52. Craig, *Knowledge and the State of Nature*.

53. Lahno, "Emotional Character," 181–82.

54. Jones, "Trust as an Affective Attitude," 4. I'd suggest that the converse is also true: if I am trusted, I can expect that the one trusting will be motivated (constrained) by the thought that I am trustworthy.

55. David Hume, *A Treatise of Human Nature*, 2nd ed, ed. P. Nidditch (Oxford: Clarendon Press, 1978), 180.

56. Kristina Rolin, "Gender and Trust in Science," *Hypatia* 17, no. 4 (2002): 95–118. She is motivated by reasons similar to those prompting Jane Braaten's insistence that intellectual virtues should include virtues concerned with community, although her focus is different.

57. Rolin, "Gender and Trust," 108.

58. Rolin, "Gender and Trust," 111.

59. Patricia J. Williams, *The Alchemy of Race and Rights: Diary of a law professor* (Cambridge MA: Harvard University Press, 1991), 146–47.

60. For an account of pedagogical authority in classrooms see R. Hanrahan and L. Antony "Because I Said So: Toward a Feminist Theory of Authority," *Hypatia* 20, no. 4 (2005): 59–79.

61. Rolin, "Gender and Trust," contains a very thorough explanation of how John Hardwig's view of trust in science is flawed by precisely this neglect.

62. This example is also discussed in my "Trust and the Curse of Cassandra."

63. Thanks to Graeme Marshall for making the significance of this point clear to me.

64. Linda Zagzebski has suggested that Cassandra will end up lacking knowledge, and according to the myth, she goes mad. This reinforces the claim that recognition from fellow epistemic agents is essential for maintenance of epistemic agency. Linda Zagzebski, "Epistemic Trust," *Philosophy in the Contemporary World* 10, no. 2 (2003): 113–17.

65. Code, *Epistemic Responsibility*, 193.

66. Rae Langton, "Epistemic Injustice: Power and the Ethics of Knowing by Miranda Fricker," *Hypatia* 25, no. 2 (2010): 459–64.

67. Fricker, "Epistemic Injustice," 170.

68. Fricker, *Epistemic Injustice*, 88.

69. Note that the replaceable source would be unproblematic if epistemic agents were mere instrumental sources for one another.

70. Kristina Rolin shows that this consideration requires knowledge seeking enterprises like science to take social arrangements into account where these affect who is considered trustworthy. Rolin, "Gender and Trust."

71. Fricker, "Epistemic Injustice," 172.

72. Braaten, "A Feminist Reassessment."

Chapter Three

Institutional Epistemic Dependence

The field of epistemic dependence contains more than the relatively informal and unstructured informational transactions that take place between individual epistemic agents. Epistemic dependence also has institutional dimensions: there are systematic ways of organizing flows of information between expert and specialist groups and non-expert members of a community. What might be called an epistemic economy raises distinct questions about epistemic interdependence and the values that do or might underpin our shared knowledge-related practices. Here, as with knowledge interactions at the individual level, a range of values are in play, which are not reducible to knowledge increase. I will argue that at the level of the division of epistemic labor, ignorance, in simple, selective, and invested forms, is theoretically and practically important.

Power and status accrue to those who possess certain kinds of knowledge and knowledge in some domains tends to extend authority beyond those domains. Ignorance and knowledge interact in various and complex ways: it is not the case that an absence or lack of knowledge will match a corresponding lower level of power. Ignorance, in particular, invested ignorance, can also entrench power and authority, just as knowledge can. The power associated with knowledge can become a power to deem others ignorant, and the ascription of ignorance becomes a factor that justifies excluding some persons from authoritative positions, or enables experts to act and decide on others' behalf. At the same time, simple ignorance is inherent in the division of epistemic labor, precisely because some know what others do not. Thus, the division of epistemic labor distributes both knowledge and ignorance. Understanding types and patterns of knowledge distribution demands understanding both selective and invested ignorance, and also a revaluation of simple ignorance. If a knower cooperates with another only by remedying simple ignorance, the roles of experts are limited to discovery and disclosure, both of which should (on the assumption that increasing knowledge is always good) be maximized. Instead, experts are properly discreet and discriminating—they consider what inquiries to pursue, how much to tell and who to inform. Thus there is a *prima facie* case for ignorance to have a positive as well as a structural role in an account of the division of epistemic labor. This is both because of the role of ignorance in trust and discretion, and because the proper acknowledgment of ignorance is essential to exercising some kinds of expertise responsibly. Excessive love of knowledge treats ignorance as best eliminated, and can encourage what Marilyn Frye[1] and others have identified as arrogance. Ignorance is a theoretically indispensable concept at the institutional level of epistemic dependence.

THE DIVISION OF EPISTEMIC LABOR

In contemporary industrialized societies such as Australia, New Zealand, Canada, and the United States, experts provide information for the community, directly and indirectly, through research, discovery, and communication. The distribution of epistemic labor means that certain people have responsibilities and authoritative roles[2] with respect to certain matters, such as history, protocol, medicine or healing, risk management, and the like. Whether or not we consult experts directly, those of us who are not expert with respect to some domain are indirectly informed by their understandings as they influence the policies, practices, and institutions around us. So epistemic dependence is not limited to direct testimonial dependence for information. When policy makers depend on experts, all members of a community are indirectly dependent on its experts insofar as they are subject to those policies, although not all are affected in the same ways.

Ignorance's roles within any division of labor include selective ignorance, where some inquiries are pursued and others left aside, and the distribution of knowledge, as some people's expertise is complemented by others' relative ignorance. But invested ignorance can also be discerned within the division of labor, both with respect to inclusiveness within disciplines and fields of expertise, and in the ways that experts relate to a wider community.

An overvaluation of knowledge, and failure to see ignorance and its value can sustain this invested ignorance. Unreflective endorsement of a principle that recommends increasing knowledge could lead an expert or researcher to think her epistemic responsibilities were fulfilled as long as new knowledge was gained or transmitted. Kristina Rolin's critical examination of gender in science suggests otherwise.

Rolin argues that "trust in scientific testimony involves . . . trust in the community's ability to maintain the kind of social practice and culture that supports a community-wide dialogue."[3] She has in mind inclusive and responsive dialogical practices, sensitive to gender and other inequalities and to subtle discriminations: attention to the social conditions of knowledge production. Without justified confidence in such social practices, we might not be entitled to any confidence that we assign credibility via properties that really do track trustworthiness instead of via stereotypical characteristics assigned to social groups.

Rolin provides evidence of gender bias and unequal treatment that most accounts of scientific testimony don't take into account, but which show up the distinction between being trustworthy in fact, and being perceived as trustworthy and credible. Because effective criticism and recognition are significant for productive intellectual work (obviously, but not only when peer review is involved) she argues that practices of scientific communities have to promote inclusive dialogue and criticism. Systemic limits to participation for members of any group undermine the whole community's progress. Hence, Rolin argues that "a theory of scientific testimony will have to be embedded into a social epistemology that examines how communities can promote inclusive and responsive dialogue."[4]

Members of the wider community served by scientific communities need to trust those experts, hence it is important, as Rolin points out, that practices of credibility actually track trustworthiness. Responsible expertise requires critical reflection on the conditions of expert practice and research production, which can be obscured by reliance on slogans like "increasing human knowledge." Her argument rests on an instrumental value for intellectual practice—the biases she identifies "slow down the rate of advance in scientific research and contribute to a waste of resources."[5] Her analysis suggests that even if the aim is production and accumulation of knowledge, experts' responsibilities are not fulfilled as long as new knowledge is gained and transmitted—attention to the conditions under which this takes place (the epistemic, specifically scientific community) is also required.

While I agree with Rolin about the necessity for being trusted as well as trustworthy, my reasons are broader than hers. As argued in the last chapter, it isn't clear that judging one epistemic community to be better than another is merely a matter of judging that it does better at increasing knowledge for its members.[6] A community could deploy its resources to maximize widespread information, or devote them to specialized research projects, which demand confidentiality, trade secrets, and the like, or it could look to the styles and patterns of interaction and inclusion and could make epistemic improvements in any of these ways. Thus, the approach that appears most efficient or productive on one evaluative band (such as novelty) might adversely affect other dimensions (such as widespread access and dissemination), just as some kinds of intensive agriculture create environmental problems and workplace and consumer safety issues all the while producing more and cheaper meat, and thus enhancing affordable dietary options for a wide population. References to increasing "human knowledge" or "community knowledge" tend to obscure these differences[7] and such neutral language doesn't reflect the fact that scientific knowledge has proliferated despite the absence of inclusiveness and respect for all epistemic agents in some parts of the scientific community. It might be the case that a community produces more knowledge, but does so with less inclusive practices than another, if these comparisons could be made. (This might be the case if substantial resources of time and effort are required to implement inclusive strategies, or if resistance to such policies is intransigent, for example. Overcoming invested ignorance is not a matter of providing the kind of information that would remedy simple ignorance.) I argue that systematic exclusions or restrictions on some members of a community are in themselves epistemically problematic, in ways that are not restricted to their veritistic outcomes. We also need to consider what kinds of roles are available to all kinds of agents.

Epistemic injustice comprises more than exclusion from opportunities to acquire knowledge and consequent informational impoverishment (for example, being deprived of educational opportunities). It can include epistemic discredit, or absence of credence, as exemplified by the story of Cassandra and by Miranda Fricker's account of Marge Sherwood in chapter 2. Experts can fail to cultivate and enact virtues of epistemic justice, in Fricker's terms, or can fail to reflect on the nature of their epistemic community in the creative ways that Jane Braaten's feminist intellectual virtues suggest. Arrangements of the division of epistemic labor and of cognitive authority and expertise can align with or disrupt patterns of epistemic injustice, but to achieve justice, I will argue they must be guided by non-epistemophilic standards, including a non-complacent capacity for self-reflection by experts, and a critical attitude to the systems and practices that structure and enable their work.

I have argued that important epistemic virtues cannot be properly explained with a focus on individual knowers whose aim is to maximize knowledge and evidence. A comprehensive account of epistemic activities needs to begin with the various forms of interdependence and to recognize that epistemic values extend beyond knowledge proliferation. The responsibilities of knowers who work to provide explicit or background information for the community are particularly important. When we talk about knowledge as a communal activity, and recognize that knowledge is created jointly rather than individually, it becomes crucial to consider who belongs to the collectives that are making knowledge. It matters how these makers of knowledge see their own roles and associated responsibilities. If knowers are not always substitutable *qua* knowers, and different persons have different kinds and amounts of knowledge, authority, and power, then it clearly matters who is situated where with respect to knowledge and knowledge making for epistemic as well as for political reasons. These are the foundational insights of standpoint epistemology.

Who is included in the community of experts also matters because the areas of investigation experts pursue determine what material is potentially available to non-experts, and what is selectively ignored. The point here is that selective ignorance is inevitable, but which patterns of knowledge and ignorance emerge is contingent. The scope and methodology of experts' inquiries can be motivated by various reasons including pragmatic, economic, institutional, strategic, ethical, and personal factors. Government or state requirements, institutional requirements, and resources and corporate interests set many research directions. The institutions that enable knowledge production for a community are not motivated solely by simple desires to increase knowledge either from the side of individual practitioners or from bureaucratic or other influences. Invested ignorance can play important, but sometimes unnoticed roles.

EXPERTISE AND AUTHORITY

It might be assumed that the best way to arrange the division of epistemic labor would be the one that produces the maximum amount of knowledge for the community or that produces knowledge most efficiently. But what exactly is "a community's knowledge?" For example, we could conceive "a community's knowledge" to be all that which is generally accessible, such as everything that is on the public record, or to be all that is common knowledge.[8] Selecting common knowledge would seem to leave out specialized knowledge, which is precisely what is at stake when considering the epistemic division of labor. But the first option of general accessibility also faces difficulties because it is unlikely that all community members share, or have equivalent access to, a wide range of information. Problems of physical access such as geographic isolation or disability, and literacy and language competences are relevant considerations, thus it is hard to see what general accessibility amounts to. Adopting either of these assumptions obscures the structure of the division of epistemic labor and differential access to information among community members. It is not useful to analyze a community's knowledge in such a way that differences between knowers are rendered invisible.

Perhaps then, the community's knowledge comprises everything anyone knows. On this account, my most closely guarded secrets would constitute part of the "community's knowledge," even though they are unknown to any other member of the community. Restricted knowledge of specialized or secret information is compatible with this view of the "community's knowledge." But sharing information is now problematic. There needs to be some way of comparing a case where knowledge is widely shared with one in which similar information is kept secret. But on the account in question, unshared information is already part of the community's knowledge, so the account seems insensitive to what *prima facie* is an important difference.

A great deal of work would need to be done to develop a conception of what counts as the community's knowledge in order for its maximization or optimization to serve as a justification for some arrangement of epistemic labor. More importantly, it is not obvious that maximizing knowledge for a community, even if it can be given a coherent interpretation, should be the primary epistemic goal. As I have argued, cooperation between members of an epistemic community is not always served by sharing all knowledge, but is often maintained by trust, selectivity, and discretion. This also applies to the institutional division of labor.

Although taking knowledge acquisition or increase as the exclusive and ultimate goal for epistemic agents turns out to be incoherent, knowledge increases are important. My emphasis on its limitations is not a claim that knowledge generally is bad, but that epistemologically, presuming it to be good is problematic. To see that an exclusive focus on increasing knowledge must be modified, consider some strategies for acquiring knowledge that necessarily include transitional ignorance. In medical research projects whose very aim is to increase knowledge by answering specific research questions, ignorance may be crucial. In a double blind trial, neither the subjects nor the experimenters can know which subjects are taking an active drug and which a placebo. Debriefing protocols might require disclosure at some later stage, in which case, ignorance is transitional—a temporary denial of information, so a particular outcome can be achieved. But it is the ignorance of participants that is necessary for the research project, not this later disclosure. In fact, when undertaking cooperative projects, it is rarely the case that I ought to share everything that I know. Interdependence does not mean that I share *all* knowledge with *all* those with whom I am engaged in joint projects. Knowledge in practice is often far more tolerant of ignorance than traditional epistemological theory would recommend.

In cases of epistemic specialization, where some know on behalf of others, it is important that the latter can access the former's knowledge. This does not require that I must come to know exactly what an astrophysicist knows, as this would seem to defeat the purpose of the division of labor. I need to be able to borrow (part of) that knowledge or depend on it without going through the arduous process of coming to acquire full expertise myself, and without necessarily sharing all the expert's reasons and evidence for the knowledge I do obtain.[9] In fact, I will most likely acquire only a tiny amount

of the expert's knowledge, and what I learn may well be simplified or gener-
alized. Minimally, the context for anything I understand will be very different.[10] To cooperate with a non-expert, an expert needs to be sensitive to what
that person does not know as well as what she needs to know, the extent of
her ignorance, and the extent that it can be constructively remedied. But there
isn't a straightforward way to account for what epistemically responsible
experts ought to do by appealing only to increasing knowledge. That goal
turns out to be both unclear and inadequate.

Ignorance is always an aspect of the arrangement of some persons with
respect to some information in a community. It is not simply a lack or
absence of knowledge that ideally would be avoided or remedied. Knowledge increase is not the exclusive, central goal to which epistemic activities
are directed. We won't get the division of epistemic labor right by thinking of
it as the large-scale version of an individual knowledge collector. This has
already been shown to be an inadequate account of epistemic virtue.

If we include in the analysis of divisions of epistemic labor all the things
that experts do with respect not only to the production, but the distribution of
information, and the inclusion, exclusion, and recognition of others' epistemic agency, ignorance turns out to be a crucial resource for our account. If we
think not only about the production of knowledge, but also about patterns of
ignorance—not only what is known and unknown and what knowers are
achieving, but also how knowledge transactions take place, who gets to count
as knower, whose contributions are recognized, who does or does not have
access to authoritative positions within these roles and the like—we arrive at
a more complete descriptive picture and at a deeper understanding of relevant
epistemic responsibilities.

A careful examination of Alvin Goldman's account of epistemic paternalism exposes problems with taking an exclusively veritistic view of epistemic
value to define the epistemic responsibilities of experts.[11] I will show that
this account does not fully articulate the range of values involved in epistemic dependence. This is not to reject the importance of truth and knowledge (in
Goldman's terms to succumb to "veriphobia"), but to deny that veritism can
serve as the sole standard for epistemic agents, or epistemologists.

GOLDMAN AND EPISTEMIC PATERNALISM

As Goldman puts it, "[s]ocial epistemics studies the veritistic properties of
social practices or institutional rules that directly or indirectly govern communication and doxastic decision."[12] Veritistic properties are those that are
truth-conducive, and these constitute what is good within the domain of
epistemic effort. Information providers (such as news broadcasters, advertis-

ers, experts, and teachers) are supposed to act for the epistemic good of their audiences (perhaps among other non-epistemic goals). Goldman wants to provide "a general assessment of paternalistic control practices, first in terms of purely epistemic considerations, and second on more inclusive grounds"[13] so he is concerned to identify and evaluate the principles that guide the provision of evidence and information to other knowers.

While Goldman's interest in epistemic dependence including paternalistic epistemic practices suggests a community based focus, his very approach shows the influence of a traditional epistemological emphasis on individualistic knowledge: he starts with a principle purported to apply to an individual basis for belief, and extends it to interpersonal epistemic transactions. He first considers whether a principle requiring maximal evidence to be provided is generally respected in domains of epistemic authority, and he argues that it is not. He rightly rejects the suggestion that a principle requiring total evidence for individual believers (which is similar to Hall and Johnson's duty to seek more evidence) can be extended to epistemic interactions.

Goldman, then, is right about the unsustainability of a principle requiring total evidence to be provided, and about the importance of exploring the domain of social practices that control knowledge. I will show that the unacceptable aspects of his account can largely be accounted for by his misconception of the relevance of ignorance—his susceptibility to epistemophilia.

It helps to introduce Goldman's account of the transactions he regards as epistemically paternalistic with some preliminary analysis of authority and paternalism. At least two relevant types of authority can be distinguished.[14] "Authority" can mean something close to "expert," because to be an authority on a subject means to have specialized information that most people do not have. But to have authority can also mean to be in a position of authority, and to have the powers, rights, and responsibilities that go along with its exercise. Authority in this sense involves "being authorized," or having a certain kind of status and power.[15] This may accompany expertise, as in being an acknowledged or recognized expert. But one can be an unacknowledged expert, and hence be unacknowledged as an authority, or one might have authority, but not expertise.[16]

Epistemic authority exercised over others could involve either of these kinds of authority. A person can be an authority with regard to knowledge in some domain because she is an expert in that domain. Or, a person can be an authority with regard to knowledge because she is in a position to exercise control, perhaps by editing a newspaper or a website. The latter kind of authority involves authority over others' knowledge or the information available to them, but the former involves only the possession of expert knowledge that is better than the normal or ordinary standard of knowledge.

Paternalism requires the kind of authority that is related to power and control. It is a certain way of exercising authority, and has been defined as "interference with the conduct of another with their best interest in mind"[17] and as "[t]he power and authority one person or institution exercises over another to confer benefits or prevent harm for the latter regardless of the latter's informed consent."[18] As a form of authority, paternalism need not involve expertise.

Epistemic paternalism is, therefore, the exercise of control over the knowledge of others, on their behalf or in their interests. A person might occupy a position involving control over dissemination of information without being expert in the content of that information. For example, someone (a legislator) might decide to place warnings on cigarette packets, without being a medical or human behavior expert. There is relevant expertise in psychological or sociological understandings of how such warnings work, but while such experts may be consulted about the framing of the warning, those who legislate warnings on tobacco products need not be expert in this way either. Legislators need position and power, not expertise, in order to exercise paternalist epistemic authority in determining the level of disclosure required on various products. Of course, in the absence of expertise, judgments that will affect the knowledge of others might be made badly, so expertise or access to it is frequently desirable for those making paternalistic decisions. My claim is that expertise is neither necessary nor sufficient for the exercise of epistemic paternalism.

Goldman, however, recognizes no distinction between paternalism's being legitimate and its being the source of a correct judgment. He doesn't consider how expertise is conferred or attributed, and how such attributions interact with other social hierarchies. In fact, he suggests simply that expertise can legitimate paternalism, as his discussion of paternalism in education policy illustrates.[19] Goldman rightly points out that students are not standardly exposed to all information and to every viewpoint on every subject. Selectivity occurs on at least two levels: firstly, the selection of what is true and accurate information, instead of what is false; secondly, selectivity requires choosing for the curriculum content only part of what is true and relevant, since practical constraints entail that not all of this content can be included.

As examples of views that may be left out of a classroom curriculum, Goldman mentions "the flat-earth viewpoint, Ptolemaic astronomy, or astrology"[20] as well as creationism,[21] perhaps the most (in)famous and contested alternative to mainstream classroom content. These cases are very different from the selections made within the accepted canons (for example the choice of which astronomy text to prescribe), and from legal cases where the truth of certain evidence is not contested, but the material is inadmissible for some other reason. Some potentially legitimate content is omitted for (largely) pragmatic reasons; some content is omitted because it is judged not to be legitimate. Goldman argues that both are cases of epistemic paternalism because decisions are being made to control or restrict knowledge in the interests of the potential knowers and their acquisition of relevant truths.

Thus far, Goldman's analysis is reasonable. But then he turns to the question of the warrant for paternalism and makes the following claim: "Here, too, paternalism seems to be warranted on epistemic grounds. Experts on science should be allowed to decide that creationism is not a scientifically viable or serious contender, and hence should not be taught in the classroom."[22]

But even if paternalism is warranted and necessary, as it is in educational contexts, invoking expertise does not resolve a controversial issue. While it may be true that science teaching ought to follow Darwin, not Genesis, this does not follow from the fact that paternalism is warranted. It is uncontroversial that decisions about curriculum content should be made with the epistemic interests of students in mind. Such judgments are examples of legitimate epistemic paternalism, and if such decisions were made in the absence of considerations of the students' best interests, they would be made inappropriately. However, the debate between advocates of mainstream science teaching and their creationist opponents is not one between defenders of epistemic paternalism and those who would reject it. *Both* sides would claim that their strategy promotes the students' epistemic welfare and access to truth.[23] Similarly, both would cite experts to support their preferred content. Conceivably, proponents of opposing views on teaching *content* would present almost identical reasons for endorsing epistemic paternalism, and all would agree that it is warranted in this context. Invoking epistemic paternalism does not resolve the issue of what to include in science classes, it just exposes questions about whose authority should be decisive. Deference to experts may not produce the outcome that science, not religion, is taught in classrooms because part of the conflict is about which experts (or in contemporary discussions of so-called Intelligent Design, who counts as a scientific expert). Even when science is endorsed, authority and expertise are sometimes contested. Sandra Harding makes the point sharply: "'Science says . . . ,' we are told. Whose science, we can ask? The drug and cigarette companies'? The Surgeon General's? The National Institute of Health's? The science of the critics of the NIH's racism and sexism?"[24]

Goldman offers a discussion of expertise and authority which may be intended to defend his position, but in fact it shows where the confusion lies. Goldman claims that "expertise is a prime factor in the defense of epistemic paternalism. To justify any instance of such paternalism, involving a particular controller, we must have grounds for taking that agent to be an expert."[25]

But expertise is neither sufficient nor necessary for legitimate paternalism. If it were sufficient, then, in any situation where another person knew better than I, she would be entitled to make judgments on my behalf. This seems wrong. Better knowledge, or expertise, is not sufficient to warrant paternalism, and it is more plausible that Goldman regards expertise as a necessary condition of paternalism, but this is also mistaken. Paternalism is not justified by expertise, it may depend on contexts and roles, relationships, and circumstances. With respect to Goldman's example, why should classroom content be decided by scientists, instead of education bureaucrats, students, parents, teachers, religious experts, or other stakeholders such as the community in general? Expertise (or more realistically competence) may be important for making good decisions, but this is a different matter from the justified making of decisions. For example, parents exercise authority by virtue of relationship, not expertise, and do not lose the legitimacy of that authority by being inexpert. In any case, expertise is not a simple matter, and its relationship with cognitive authority should not be presumed unproblematic.

Complex decisions are often not best left to experts, and many decisions involving epistemic paternalism are of this nature. This is one reason why lay members are important participants on research ethics committees, and on guardianship boards or mental health tribunals where decisions are made about information. Goldman too hastily takes experts to be the best decision makers as well as the best information providers.

In many information exchanges, information is limited for nonpaternalistic reasons, mutually acceptable or tacitly consensual reasons. But regulations that are tacitly consensual are not really paternalistic, since in consenting, I have (arguably) decided that this arrangement of delegated authority is in my best interests. It will rarely be appropriate to aim for the total disclosure of truth, the whole truth, and nothing but the truth. But only in some cases is the controller preempting her interlocutor's capacity to decide for herself on the evidence, which is one of the differences between being dependent through delegating authority, and being subjected to epistemic paternalism or controlled for manipulative reasons.

Expertise does not suffice for paternalistic legitimacy, nor is a person in a position of legitimate paternalism necessarily there by virtue of expertise. This is clear from the fact that while a person purported to be an expert may undermine her claim to expert status by making bad judgments, the *legitimacy* of paternalistic authority would not thereby be lost (though its utility would). For example, a teacher who has the authority to decide the content for a particular session does not lose this authority by being a bad teacher, and deciding foolishly. Goldman links paternalism and expertise much too closely. Expertise may be important for assessing paternalism, but functions in relation to its effectiveness, not its legitimacy.

Expertise is one of the ways that persons are positioned differently in the epistemic domain. As Goldman notes, a proper account of this domain must acknowledge that it is marked by differences in "cognitive resources, skills and opportunities . . . different levels of expertise, by different opportunities

for information gathering, by different levels of cognitive maturity and training, and by severe time constraints."[26] It is worth considering whether Goldman's account of expertise, detached from his account of paternalism, is a
useful account of expertise *per se*. The account of paternalism is arguably a
product of epistemophilia—the idea that knowledge is good convinces Goldman that those with more knowledge (experts) can legitimately judge what
knowledge is good for others. It turns out that his account of expertise is
similarly marked.

It is dangerous to assume that increasing expert information is beneficial.
First, there are practical costs to obtaining information, and limits to what
can be usefully assimilated when a decision needs to be made. Experts in a
certain area are likely primed to organize information in certain ways, to see
and present certain features of a situation as salient. Being trained into a
certain perspective can inhibit the recognition of other factors—for example,
medical workers do not always consider alternatives to medical treatment,
and futile interventions, especially during end of life care are not rare. Some
characteristics of expertise can make it hard to negotiate outside a range of
admissible options covered by the field of expertise: problems can arise
when a narrow expertise becomes authority and any wider context is lost.

An expert is defined by Goldman as a person who either has or can
acquire true answers to core questions in the relevant domain(s). This is
expertise in its primary sense. A controller might have secondary expertise,
such as the skill to locate other experts, for example, "expertise on the question of speaker credentials" which would be possessed, for example, by the
framers of the rules applying to legal evidence.[27]

Level of expertise can be understood in either a comparative or absolute
sense, depending on whether the individual is expert absolutely or in comparison with others. Experts can be identified through their capacity to answer
questions in domains such as prediction domains, factual record domains,
repair domains, and design domains. Even novices can identify experts by
their success in such domains, Goldman claims.

Goldman is probably right about a necessary component of expertise
being the capacity to demonstrate it appropriately, for example, by answering
relevant questions, making predictions, and succeeding at practical tasks of
design or repair. He may also be right about it being "relatively easy, even
for novices or rivals, to identify expertise"[28] through examining and checking such successes, (although in many areas I doubt that I would know what
checks or expectations would be properly relevant to expertise). But Goldman fails to consider that normal practices do not include direct detection of
experts. We rely on claims to expertise, which are usually backed by complex social accreditation systems, not all of which are explicit, and not all of
which are ethically neutral. If I consult a lawyer or surgeon, or meet a
mathematician or astronomer, for example, I do not check their ability to

perform certain tasks. Nor would I necessarily know which tasks to find out about.

Goldman's account does not attend to this aspect of the division of epistemic labor. It is not merely specific or specialized content for which we rely on others, nor is it only occupants of particular (professional) roles on whom we count. There are vast dispersed networks of dependence,[29] and a large part of our reliance is indirect. Goldman's notion of expertise is problematic both because it misrepresents the ways epistemic dependence on experts actually works, and because of the use he makes of it in his account of the warrant for paternalism. I show below that Goldman's discussion of the requirement of total evidence shows that he still regards an account of epistemic interactions as derivable from an individualistic account. Goldman neglects the depth of epistemic dependence because he remains compelled by the image of knowing for oneself, and ignores the value of ignorance.

GOLDMAN'S REQUIREMENT OF TOTAL EVIDENCE

Goldman uses the principle of the "requirement of total evidence" (RTE) as an "expository heuristic to introduce the topic of epistemic paternalism."[30] The strong form of the principle states that the best cognitive judgment demands the use of all evidence available to the agent at minimal cost.[31] This principle is, Goldman states, popular "in epistemology and the philosophy of science,"[32] and in fact in many theories it appears as the main principle governing knowledge-seeking activities. However, by focusing on examples of knowledge interchange, Goldman shows that those who are in a position to paternalistically control the knowledge status of others do not use such a principle.[33] For example, educators who have a clear motivation to develop good cognitive judgments in students do not (and could not) achieve this aim by providing *all* the available information.

Goldman distinguishes a weak and a strong form of the principle of the requirement of total evidence:

> (W-RTE) A cognitive agent X should always fix his beliefs or subjective probabilities in accordance with the total evidence in his possession at the time.

The strong form of the principle adds a requirement for the acquisition of evidence, which is absent from the weak form:

> (S-RTE) A cognitive agent X should collect and use all available evidence that can be collected and used (at negligible cost).[34]

The weak form demands only that an agent make use of all the relevant information she has, but the strong form imposes an obligation to use all available information, at least when it can be obtained at minimal cost. Goldman takes the strong form to be acceptable, and this is initially plausible. In at least some contexts, decision-makers should probably not assume their current information state is adequate, and there are often things we should know more about, for example, I should check the safety instructions, or read signs.

Goldman specifies the interpersonal version of RTE in relation to control of evidence: if Y controls the availability of evidence to X, then, "Y should make available to X all the evidence that is subject to his (Y's) control."

> (C-RTE) If agent X is going to make a doxastic decision concerning question Q, and agent Y has control over the evidence that is provided to X, then, from a purely epistemic point of view, Y should make available to X all of the evidence relevant to Q which is (at negligible cost) within Y's control.[35]

Goldman argues that that the control version of the requirement of total evidence principle (C-RTE) is unacceptable, and sets out to show that many existing provisions and practices contravene it. He identifies authorities who operate paternalistically, or control information for others' good. He finds examples in law, education, and broadcasting regulation. Such decisions, which are made by authorities in the interests of other cognitive agents, do not comply with C-RTE.

As it stands, Goldman's version of C-RTE is *prima facie* implausible. Many kinds of interaction ranging from such simple activities as playing cards to complex business negotiations could not take place if such a condition were imposed, that is, if no one treated any information as confidential. Goldman might respond that these kinds of interaction are not primarily epistemic, so it makes sense that other considerations would prevail. This is fine, but now it is necessary to find a way of distinguishing between contexts that are primarily epistemic and those that are not. But we lack such a distinction, and without it, it is difficult to identify any circumstances in which a principle that refers only to providing total evidence might be applicable.

It is noteworthy that Goldman's generation of the C-RTE principle involves an assumption that a principle that (apparently) guides autonomous knowledge activities can simply be transferred to a domain of epistemic interactions. However, it is not obviously a good idea to treat individual knowledge-seeking as the model for interpersonal knowledge exchanges: indeed, the reverse might be more plausible. In most cases, the acquisition of knowledge is an interpersonal matter and perfectly autonomous knowledge activities are few and far between and quite difficult to isolate. It is usually better to use the standard or common case to explain the less ordinary situation, and in the epistemic context, this means explaining individual knowledge in social terms, not the other way around.

In any case, the nature of obligations is not normally such that a principle guiding my behavior entails a principle requiring other persons' cooperation. The fact that I should work carefully and rigorously on my research project does not mean that others are universally obliged to assist me (although there might be a minimal requirement not to thwart or subvert my legitimate activities). Similarly, the fact (if it is fact) that I should attend to the available evidence in making a judgment does not oblige others to provide me with evidence. This may be so in some cases, but is not universally so. We, in fact, expect others to exercise discretion which may reflect previous commitments, tacit or explicit trust conditions, respect for another's privacy or other reasons for non-disclosure. Someone concerned for my epistemic interests might be concerned for my intellectual development, for my manifesting an unconditioned and perhaps creative response, for my learning to ask relevant questions, and so on. Evidence is not the only epistemic focus.

Goldman's remarks about the nature of epistemic interests that are to be considered by a regulator of news services are worth examining because they reveal his view of epistemic value. He argues that simplification of both the content of issues and of the range of possible interpretations can "reduce the number of truths an audience has an opportunity to acquire"[36] but this is offset by the tradeoffs of avoiding confusion and error, and the increased audience size for simpler information. Simplification can thus be justified on account of epistemic paternalism, as being in the epistemic interests of the audience, so we are not confused by excessive information or discouraged, even baffled, by incomprehensible complexity. The accessibility of simpler information to a greater audience "may mean that more true beliefs (for example, belief tokens) are acquired through the simplified set of messages than would otherwise be the case."[37] It seems correct that an audience may be better able to grasp less detailed information, but it is much less obvious that the only benefit lies in an increase of true beliefs. Educative functions are much broader than just feeding information.

Goldman argues that fecundity (the number of persons acquiring true beliefs) is a genuine epistemic value. It is unclear whether Goldman means that all beliefs are equal, or whether there are differences when different persons acquire beliefs. He does not explain how to compare fecundity with other measures of beliefs, and exactly how the trade-off of simpler for more numerous beliefs functions. It is also a little unclear exactly whose interests are those being considered by paternalistic regulators. It might be the current news-viewing audience, or the potential audience, or the community in general, and decisions might vary according to whose interests are prioritized.

Goldman equates epistemically valuable outcomes with true belief and error avoidance. He defends this position and argues that other candidates for epistemic value like (Mill's conception of) deeper or livelier impressions of truth, or argumentative skills, can be cashed out as grasp of truths, or the enhanced capacity to grasp truths.[38] However, there are problems with these criteria for epistemically valuable outcomes. When looking at epistemic community and epistemic authority, it is essential to have a less individualistic account of epistemic value. My epistemic welfare includes not only the beliefs I currently hold, but also those to which I have relatively easy access, through others' expertise, among other things. This involves not just the presence of information somewhere in my community, but my access to it, perhaps via libraries and internet search engines. I need to cultivate capacities to use them, and the confidence to do so, and these require a broader scope of epistemic agency. The division of labor means that I can rely on authority, not just that I can acquire further evidence. But since reliance is not mere passive reception, attention needs to be given to how a community ensures the competence of epistemic agents. This requires attention to credibility, trust, and the like.

Overall, then, Goldman's efforts to incorporate questions about paternalism and the sharing of information into epistemological discussions are flawed both by his epistemophilia and by his failure to recognize how much an interpersonal epistemology must diverge from individualistic models. It is not sufficient to take atomistic subjects posited by such a model and add them together and make a composite of their interactions. The interactions must be taken as primary, because subjects and their knowledge are constituted in important ways by these interactions. Such considerations reveal the need for a new account of knowledge, and a different evaluation of ignorance.

I argued earlier against Hall and Johnson's claims that the only appropriate epistemological goal is to know all and only truths and that we have an associated duty always to seek more evidence. I have also shown that Goldman's account of epistemic paternalism and his explanation of its warrant fail due to his misunderstanding of the nature and source of epistemic authority and his confusion of authority with expertise. This misunderstanding of expertise derives from the supposition that it does not matter who has knowledge, because it is the same for everyone. Consequently, the knowledge of experts is taken to legitimate their judgments on behalf of others, since anyone with that knowledge would judge in the same way. The presumed uniformity of knowledge produces a distorted account of epistemic dependence.

Goldman, like Hall and Johnson, is mistaken about the processes of exchanging knowledge, even though he has explicitly set out to investigate some of the characteristics of an epistemic community. Taking ignorance seriously leads us to a very different view of knowledge where the positions, contexts, and diversity of knowers are central features.

RESPONSIBLE EXPERTISE

Experts can inform accurately, but fail to be fully responsible by not reflecting on their role, in particular its creative and constructive dimensions. If they treat other members of the community merely as repositories for their discoveries or as objects for knowing about, they will be epistemically irresponsible: thinking that all an expert needs to do is to know and tell, distorts and obscures responsible practice. A culture of expertise can incorporate reflexive critical practice, or discourage it. It is worth noting here, as Helen Longino points out, that experts and other knowledge producers can (and perhaps usually do) belong to multiple cognitive communities, and hence being an expert does not preclude access to external critical perspectives, as these can be present in a single knower.[39] However, this does not guarantee that the critical perspectives will be engaged, and there can be incentives towards or against openness and compartmentalism. Some kinds of expert groups are less open to criticism than others, and it will be a contingent and local matter whether the presumed authority of expertise is easy to contest. Views such as Goldman's that align authority and expertise can de-legitimate criticism from outside the acknowledged expert group.

The extent and complex nature of expert responsibility can be seen by examining how it can fail. Communicating and sharing knowledge are crucial elements of expert responsibility and as well as being knowledgeable, experts need to exercise judgment in making what they know available to others. Discretion motivates a set of characteristic behaviors towards knowledge and other knowers that include forbearing to seek certain kinds of knowledge, and not disclosing certain kinds of information. Usually "discretion" refers to the limits on how much personal information concerning self or others is shared, but it can also apply to the exercise of judgment with respect to experts' inquiry and disclosure. There are at least two reasons why discretion has a moral aspect: first, the information is not neutral, but often deals with matters of potential moral significance; and second, discreet and indiscreet behaviors often involve choices about how to treat other persons. There are clear ethical reasons to be discreet and trustworthy, including respect for persons, respect for privacy, and avoiding causing harm or unhappiness to others. Epistemic considerations also have a central role.

Discretion can mean that I have knowledge, but I choose not to share it. It is a character trait or disposition that requires cultivation, and is one that we would expect a competent epistemic player to have and maintain. Experts can be discreet by exercising appropriately cautious disclosure, and it is particularly important that they do so, since an excess of specialist information to a non-expert can be counter productive, impeding rather than aiding understanding. The epistemic dimension of discretion includes identifying kinds of knowledge, contexts, and relations, areas and degrees of disclosure, and appropriate responses to interlocutors. This dimension of epistemic practice is not restricted to ethical contexts: such skills are important in almost all exchanges of knowledge. I exercise epistemic discretion when judging how much information to impart when asked for directions, as well as when discussing a mutual friend in general conversation. If I were to describe in architecturally accurate detail every building you will pass on your way to the post office, you might never find your way there, but I would have informed you truthfully and accurately. If, when we discover an acquaintance in common, I share with you my familiarity with her extensive record collection by listing recording details for every song title, I might bore you, but my error is not moral. The appropriate degree of detail is given in some cases by epistemic, not moral considerations, and the judgment involved means discretion is exercised. The point here is not to deny that moral considerations can be relevant to the disclosure of information, but to show that epistemic considerations also have a central role.

Experts also control the information available to the wider community through deciding what inquiries are undertaken. Within a discipline, experts can determine areas of ignorance because by deciding what knowledge to pursue, we effectively decide to leave other areas unexplored. One commentator has described the process of scientific inquiry in this way:

> Because of the structuring of science, the tracks of knowledge could also be considered from another perspective as tracks of ignorance, because a particular knowledge line defines a particular area of exploration as valid and leaves the area outside this demarcation unexplored. . . . A knowledge track or tube is by training of the scientist, given tradition and practice, as much programmed to structured ignorance as to structured knowledge. [40]

Taking scientific investigation in a particular direction of exploration has the result that certain tracks are followed, while others are ignored. So we can understand the process of scientific discovery as one of selectivity and just as we might ask what has been learned, we might ask what has not been investigated. Failures to include female subjects in medical, psychological, and pharmaceutical research provide a range of cases where such questions are important. Remedying ignorance sometimes requires a critical perspective to identify what has been left out. As Rolin argues, cultivating this kind of attitude in scientific practices demands a civil and inclusive attitude to all participants. [41]

The metaphor of tracks of knowledge suggests an expanse of ignorance, but if we just ask which knowledge has been acquired, and which ignorance eliminated, we might mistakenly assume that the world of information is static, and therefore we can just go back and fill in gaps that were left. This image obscures the ways that professional knowledge is constructed. Knowledge production is not a simple matter of experts setting out to undertake research and make discoveries through collections and assessments of data. This can be seen most easily in, but is not restricted to the social sciences, where academics and professionals both discover the content or data and develop the concepts and methods of the discipline. In Kathryn Addelson's words: "[t]he professionals define the nature of the subjects and the activity, and they define what is to be included as environment and what is to be ignored and hidden."[42] Researchers not only "find" and collect evidence, but also determine what counts as evidence, and how that evidence is to be categorized. By deciding what to pursue and what to leave unexplored, researchers and other professionals decide the scope and boundaries of the discipline.

The creativity of experts is clearest when they present a revisionary challenge to the mainstream perspectives of a discipline, for example, when feminists contest dominant assumptions in philosophy, science, or history. It is a creative practice to redefine the parameters of the discipline, but it is equally, although less obviously, creative to maintain their standard constructions. Whether they maintain conservative borders, or radically renegotiate them, researchers and experts have the authority to decide what becomes knowledge, and thus to define knowledge and ignorance within a domain.

Addelson advocates a mode of responsibility with broad scope: she says, "[b]eing intellectually responsible requires, for professionals like myself, devising theories and practices that can make it explicit what the collective activity is and what some important outcomes of the activity might be."[43] In discussing the human genome project, she states:

> there is the general issue of the authority of the researchers in defining what we are, who we are, and how we should live—not in words or empty theories, but in ways that will be implemented in the health care, educational, and legal systems. Using DNA testing in the courts, labelling people deviant by genetic testing is a powerful contribution to the definition of how we should live. My point here is not to say the scientists involved in the genome project are promoting false theories. I'm saying rather that they are abstracting the experimental situation of their research out of the larger collective action that includes themselves. It is not that their work isn't "true," it is that they run a very serious risk of not exercising moral and intellectual responsibility.[44]

As Addelson points out, there are both moral and intellectual considerations here. On this account, the difference between an expert or professional and others is not only that one has a greater quantity of knowledge and the others are in a position of dependence. Delivering truths to the community does not exhaust the responsibility of experts. Those who are epistemically responsible in Addelson's terms need to be conscious of the role of professional knowledge-makers, and recognize their participation in exercising authority. They need to practice virtues of epistemic cooperation and those required by epistemic justice.

The history of midwives, as discussed by Vrinda Dalmiya and Linda Alcoff, is one example of how definitions of knowledge and ignorance can emerge. They record that the responsibility for assisting women in childbirth was taken over by trained physicians while at the same time "women were systematically excluded from entering universities, medical schools, and training clinics as these began to arise."[45] The authors argue that this is a case of privileging officially sanctioned knowledge over knowledge based in experience and empathy, and knowledge gained through practical skills and competences.[46] As medical expertise increased, so did the authority of official practitioners to both define what counted as medical knowledge (excluding the experience of midwives) and to control the conditions for training new practitioners (midwives were not retrained to use new information).

The power of professionals, experts, and knowledge makers to affect conditions for the whole community, combined with the social advantages that accrue to those engaged in knowledge production, highlight the importance of questions about the representativeness of the class of knowledge makers. Notoriously, experts tend to come from privileged social groups. Sandra Harding notices the exclusion of members of marginalized groups from high-status epistemic roles, and advocates their inclusion in knowledge-making processes in order to generate less distorted and more strongly objective research practices and outcomes. She accepts that knowledge ought not to be distorted by particular interests, but proposes a politically informed approach to eliminating such distortions.[47] Harding claims, for example, that including representatives from a greater range of social locations in research projects will produce more critical questioning and thus maximize or strengthen objectivity. We become more objective by paying more, not less, attention to political issues and social concerns. Harding's analysis shows minimally that, given the association of expertise and social privilege, we cannot assume that nothing over and above superior knowledge makes some people experts on behalf of everyone else. Attention to the real ineliminable ignorance of professionals replaces attention to the presumed eliminable ignorance of nonexperts through a recognition of diverse perspectives and the acknowledgment that both knowledge and ignorance are constructed and created products.

These considerations suggest that responsible expertise demands reflecting on disciplinary practices and the constitution of expert groups. It is important that the diversity of a group of knowledge makers is similar to that of their wider community as some advantages will accrue from a representative group, for example, it is likely that a more complete range of diverse perspectives will be included. Critical content and openness to such social dimensions of expertise have the potential to effect what is done as well as to change who is doing it.

Kathryn Addelson offers an analysis of epistemic authority that is intended to explain both how the production of knowledge is a collective project, and how professionals can think responsibly about their practice of authority. She develops this analysis keeping in view an understanding that truth, knowledge, and expertise are embedded in our social practices, within specialist disciplines and everyday activities. It is not the case that professionals gain pure information—neutral knowledge of an unchanging world— or that this same knowledge could in principle be discovered by anyone committed to that pursuit. Addelson's account explains why knowers are not interchangeable—their particular contextual characteristics play a constant role in what each individual or group comes to know.

RESPONSIBILITY, EXPERTISE, AND IGNORANCE

The idea that what gets developed and presented as knowledge is partially what certain people and groups define and promote does not make knowledge or its pursuit worthless, nor should the recognition of the social aspects of knowledge acquisition undermine the legitimate authority of experts in many contexts. The point is not that we ought never to consult a medical specialist, but that we ought to be cautious about regarding such an expert as representing a neutral and impartial discipline and its *purely* scientific body of knowledge. Similarly, a theory of knowledge should not rely on such an uncritical view of expertise—that some members of a community simply know best. This is not to say that we can't compare who knows more or less on some topic, merely that this does not suffice as an account of expertise, authority, and the division of epistemic labor. An important corollary of this analysis is that it shows why non-experts who are comparatively ignorant can actually have an epistemic advantage, because they are not blinkered by the training that is typical of the expert's discipline. Training can make certain things natural and obvious that outsiders would not take for granted; in a sense, experts in a given discipline form an epistemic community that can reinforce without questioning frameworks and perceptions that shape what can be known within that discipline. The importance of lay members on ethics committees and boards overseeing professional groups such as nurses reflects the importance of diverse perspectives that can come from those outside the disciplines in question.

This analysis of epistemic authority reveals ignorance as not merely a lack of certain specialist information. Non-experts can bring an unconditioned perspective that can expose what is taken for granted within a discipline. Furthermore, although expertise depends on others not knowing, the responsibilities of experts are not exhausted by the provision of information. I qualify as an expert only when my skill or information is in some way special. Expertise only makes sense where some know what most others do not. But if my expertise, as in the case of many professionals and academics, also carries with it the power to determine what else counts as knowledge or understanding, as a member of such a select group I can participate in and maintain the system of cognitive authority, and also decide who else qualifies as having knowledge. This can produce the kind of distortion that worries Sandra Harding, especially when it masquerades as neutrality. Expert practice also imposes a kind of ignorance upon authorities by delimiting what is investigated and by setting up what is taken for granted and what is in question. On Addelson's analysis, experts are not responsible only for knowing about and on behalf of others, but their responsibility further involves acknowledgment of how others' understandings are included or excluded.

Experts, then, determine how both knowledge and ignorance are constructed in a community. Experts on knowledge, a group which includes but is not restricted to epistemologists, have the potential to influence how knowledge is understood and regulated within a community. How experts see themselves with respect to others' ignorance can vary between an attitude that "they lack the knowledge that we have," or "they have different perspectives that perhaps we ought to take into account" or even "my expertise may make me ignorant of other things and hence generates my dependence on others, not just their dependence on me."

The conception of knowledge as a collective enterprise demands acknowledgment of the role of ignorance. Under the still dominant view of knowledge as the supreme and exclusive epistemic value, ignorance is simply a regrettable lack of knowledge. Evidence may as yet be undiscovered, but it is out there, and in principle anyone can get it. It does not really matter who acquires knowledge, because any investigation would yield the same results. Any failure to acquire or to share knowledge indicates an epistemic vice. Thus, ignorance both can and should be eliminated or minimized. Reliance on others as sources of knowledge is relatively unproblematic, and occupying the position of expert demands only attention to factual accuracy. Epistemic obligations and responsibilities are reduced to dealing rigorously with facts and evidence. If, as an expert, I am presumed to be responsible only to the facts, then so as long as my research is properly carried out, I am fulfilling my responsibilities. Such a view fails to acknowledge the relations between persons that are central to the construction and dissemination of knowledge. Furthermore, adherence to this view obscures the responsibilities of a knowledge-maker who does not merely discover, but also enacts truth. Harding's program of including representatives from marginalized groups in knowledge production is one way that a revised understanding of an epistemological concept like objectivity has implications for appropriate knowledge making practices. This recognition motivates a different understanding of professional responsibility and a different attitude to epistemic authority.[48] An account of epistemic responsibility that emerges from theorizing knowers as cooperative agents rather than knowledge collectors also gives an epistemic justification for including others as knowers: failure to credit and acknowledge other knowers can be a vice. Kristina Rolin, as noted in chapter 2, argues for norms of civility, "that guarantee all members of the community are entitled to be heard and to be responded to respectfully."[49] Her argument rightly recognizes that the epistemic welfare of agents is not simply a matter of their possession of or access to truths. Most members of an epistemic community need to have the skills both to inform and to be informed, to ask for and to provide justifications, to identify and to embody authority. Not only am I one among many in my epistemic world, my epistemic environment is not uniform. In the context of the division of epistemic labor, the emphasis on expert possession of knowledge has obscured the importance of a broad range of virtues. As shown in Chapter 1, being a competent potential knower means, not independence, but admitting the importance and utility for me of other people's knowledge, and being able to identify appropriate persons or products to depend on. Being an expert requires complementary virtues of responding to the epistemic agency of those who depend on me in a way that recognizes participation and cooperation as aspects of their epistemic welfare.

If members of some social groups are excluded from the privileged knowledge making groups, those practicing the kind of responsibility defended here will notice it as an epistemic as well as a political concern.[50] Understanding these aspects of epistemic responsibility is helped by a constructive attitude to ignorance. My epistemic responsibilities cannot be reduced to the elimination of ignorance and promotion of knowledge and my responsibilities as a knowledge-maker include a sensitivity to the ways that expertise can exclude other possibilities of knowledge. Knowledge is made legitimate by fitting it into a system or order, and those who occupy positions at higher levels of the (professional or bureaucratic) structure exercise the power of legitimating knowledge. Those with high status in an institutionalized knowledge hierarchy can know about and for others. Their practices can include the treatment of other persons as credible and authoritative knowers in their own right, or simply as objects of knowledge.

Miranda Fricker's analysis of epistemic justice suggests the kind of virtue that experts should display, requiring them to attend to power relations between parties, to their own social identity and that of those they seek to know and/or to tell. The relevant virtues mitigate against unwarranted discredit, and hence against failure to acquire information through testimony, and demand justice, recognition, and respect for other members of the epistemic community.

EMPATHY AND EPISTEMIC AUTHORITY

Ignorance has a particularly important role when other persons are the objects of knowledge and knowledge claims. As Lorraine Code argues with respect to empathic knowledge, certain expert practices can be imperialist.[51] By this, Code means that the space of another's feeling is taken to be available for the expert's description, understanding and knowledge, so the expert becomes the authority on what is felt. "Indeed, one of the indicators of privilege in a hierarchically structured society is the capacity to act as a 'surrogate knower': one who can put himself in the place of anyone else and know *for* them what their best interests are."[52] Such tendencies can be resisted by making explicit the value of ignorance in empathic expertise.

Empathy is part of relating to other knowers as epistemic agents in their own right, not just sources of information whose capacities for epistemic agency are instrumentally useful. Empathy is a way of knowing how someone feels that is essential for intimate relationships, and also important in contexts of professional knowledge such as counseling.[53] Acknowledging the credibility of the person known is important, even when the one knowing through empathy is an expert, such as a counselor, or psychologist. The person known must always be seen as potentially credible. Indeed, there should be a presumption in favor of her capacity to *say* how it is, not in favor of the expert's ability to *judge* or determine how it is. If I know through empathy, I have to be open to the person's denial that I know—if she says "no, you don't know how I feel," I have to take that seriously. So the virtues of acknowledgment and humility are important qualities for an empathic knower. It is not that everything claimed by a person known through empathy must be taken as final, because empathy allows for reciprocity between the knower and the known person and for first person fallibility. But when knowing through empathy, it is essential to consider the person known as one with her own perspective, not just different information, and not as a person who, if she had the expert's information, would think about it in the same way.[54]

Engaging with others in a properly empathic way leaves them a space to contribute their knowledge, even to develop it. To an extent, even an expert's empathic knowledge must always be provisional, revisable, and modifiable. That is to say, in empathy there is a space of ignorance—my empathic knowledge is always incomplete. In empathy, I have to see the other as a knower with her own perspective, one I have to strive (and might fail) to appreciate. The empathic process is open-ended, and when I claim that "I know just how you feel" this is not true once and for all, with the facts of the matter completely settled.

Epistemic humility shows the importance of attention to ignorance. Treating a person merely as evidence guarantees failure at empathy. An epistemic vice of arrogance[55] corresponds to the virtue of successful empathy—not just because I might arrogantly get it wrong, or because I might be morally arrogant, but because I can be epistemically arrogant. Even though I have true and justified beliefs, I may treat another person wrongly not (only) in an ethical sense, but epistemically, by not fully crediting her as a knower.[56] This includes my realization of the limits of what I know, the provisionality of my knowledge of another person, and the importance of remembering that another may know more than I do even though I am the expert in this context. This is important with respect to expertise since an expert, precisely because of her status, presumed objectivity, and power, may find the epistemic humility that is intrinsic to empathy in tension with that very expertise. This way of understanding empathy shows the limits of the idea that an expert's knowledge can be simply shared or made public. Successful empathy might depend on confidentiality, and empathic knowers are not interchangeable.

Ignorance is an ineliminable structural part of the division of epistemic labor. The same attitudes to knowledge that encourage its coalescence with authority and status tend to come from a dismissive attitude to ignorance. Epistemic authority is significant precisely because ignorance is also pervasive. Without some persons being ignorant, it would make no sense that others were expert. Ignorance, however, is not always based on a contrast between the one who knows and the one who is ignorant. One of the important roles of knowers is the confirmation and recognition of what others know. I may lack information and be called ignorant, or recognition may be withheld from me, and I am ascribed ignorance, in cases of invested ignorance. Some ignorance is the denial, not the lack of knowledge, and some ignorance is not an epistemic vice at all. When ignorance is part of respectful, empathic, or trusting engagement with another knower, it is part of epistemic virtue, and epistemic authority needs to incorporate this kind of epistemic virtue as well as that associated with information.

Pragmatists share a similar view of a space for openness in knowledge. "Since knowing, for pragmatists is a social endeavor and is dependent on experiences, it is always conditional because a new voice may bring a new interpretation of the question."[57] This involves a role for ignorance—since whatever is known is provisional, there is always a space of ignorance, not as a gap to be filled in to achieve completeness, but always open-ended. Recognizing this role is important because it replaces thinking about a virtuous epistemic agent as a successful collector with seeing them as interdependent inquirers.

Thinking about ignorance shows how to challenge some assumptions about knowledge which back up the alliance of knowledge and power: knowledge is always good, more knowledge is better, information and factual gaps should be filled and knowledge is neutral. A serious consideration of epistemic dependence within an epistemic community reveals that each of these assumptions must be modified. Knowledge and ignorance have ethical and political implications in practice, and so do theoretical understandings of knowledge and ignorance.

Epistemic responsibility cannot be reduced to maximizing the collection of facts and evidence. Recognition of the other persons as knowers and one's role with respect to other epistemic agents are also important. It is not the case that those who do not share the experts' view ought to have their ignorance replaced by information, nor that the existence of alternate perspectives cancels the experts' claim to knowledge. Ignorance and knowledge are not always mutually exclusive, because of the selectivity involved in knowledge making and diverse perspectives. Epistemic humility can be a virtue, because it cannot be assumed that an expert judgment captures all the important facets of a situation, nor expresses the only right way to understand it. Not only are the understandings of the situation socially generated, but the very authority of professionals itself is also a created product. This reverses the idea that authority is grounded in knowledge, and that the authority of experts is therefore a natural result of their superior information.

Automatically valuing knowledge over ignorance seems to support the view that expert knowers deserve some special status, because their work is highly valuable, and, presumably, valuable in a way that advantages all persons. Ignorance appears in this structure of expertise only as the devalued opposite to knowledge. But as I have argued, the best epistemological arguments do not support the automatic valuation of knowledge over ignorance. The ways that expertise makes some persons superior to others on the basis of (real or deemed) knowledge and ignorance are not the only ways in which ignorance has to be recognized. Ignorance is significant because we cannot presume that epistemic responsibility requires sharing all knowledge, nor that knowledge naturally implies any kind of special authority.

Factors relevant to who knows best include the domain in question, and whether it is one demanding a high degree of accuracy, or where approximation can be tolerated (or is even preferable), for what purpose the knowledge is intended (including who is seeking to know) and to what extent the question is about authority. I may get a different sense of a friend's health situation from a family member, a nurse, or a medical specialist. If I have to decide who is the best person to ask, then a great deal depends on what I want to know, and on what I can expect to be disclosed to me. A consideration such as who might be the source of *most* information or evidence is not suitable to guide my pursuit of knowledge in this context. The same roles and connections are not equivalent for all epistemic agents or for every context.

The status that accrues to some kinds of profession is supported by ideas about the value of knowledge, and the nature of knowledge. Expertise is not just a necessary consequence of the division of labor, some doing intellectual work while others work in different fields as artists, primary producers or child carers. There is a challenge to avoid a pernicious kind of "epistemic obliviousness" to which experts may be tempted. This is not the overlooking of evidence, but a failure to attend to the knowledge of the (non-expert) people with whom the professional is engaged, which in the most extreme form becomes treating them merely as objects, not subjects, of knowledge. A distorted epistemological perspective may also generate a kind of obliviousness to the actual practices in which the expert is engaged and to her associated responsibilities. The best response to the recognition of such ignorance is not to patch it up with knowledge, to make oneself more informed, as an epistemophiliac might recommend, but to maintain a responsibility that incorporates epistemic humility, an understanding of ignorance, and an avoidance of epistemic vices such as discredit.

Ignorance is not only a negative thing, consisting of gaps to be filled with knowledge. As I have shown with respect to empathic knowledge, to know well in some contexts requires that even experts understand their knowledge as incomplete so that there is space for negotiating with others. Ignorance is always implicated in empathic knowledge, and accepting the limits of knowledge is an important dimension of epistemic responsibility.

Power, authority, and expertise need to be understood in *epistemic* terms as well as from political and moral perspectives. The epistemic implications of the division of epistemic labor can be considered separately from the ethical considerations. While in practice, these dimensions are deeply entangled, looking at them from either the ethical and political or the epistemic side can help to discern some aspects of what goes on. To understand her own activities, the knower must see herself as engaged within a complex community, in which knowers as well as knowledge are made, and even unmade. This needs to inform her sense of what it is to be a knower on whom others depend. Treating the knowledge of experts as neutral, impartial, and constrained only by factual accuracy leaves important epistemic considerations out of the analysis. Keeping ignorance in mind is necessary to understand the responsibility of epistemic authorities.

Researchers and experts are socially embedded, and it is part of our responsibility to consider our own professional perspective, and the framework within which we are operating. Can I be an effective expert, one who tells others, purely in virtue of my own capacities and the content of what I know? The cases of Cassandra and Marge tell us not; a testimonial act is not complete unless there is uptake. The achievement and exercise of expertise is to some extent patterned according to the orderings of social groups, and can entrench or challenge existing social structures. This is not to say the status quo is all bad, and change is always good—as the example of midwives shows. Rather, responsible experts may need to think beyond the truths of their claims because development of theoretical frameworks by experts can inform directly or indirectly various standards of practice and because the experts' view may become the one used for social governance and ordering. Think of the effects of identifying and contesting medical paternalism.

This issue of experts' responsibly acknowledging their own social position is of critical concern to feminist theorists as for example, they think about research practices involving members of less privileged groups, such as indigenous peoples and refugees, and approaches to understanding social oppression generally. White US feminists have faced criticisms for taking their own middle-class position to represent all women, when as bell hooks, for example, points out, a concern with the limitations of a life focused on domestic responsibilities is less important to many women than fair working conditions.[58] Thinking through expertise from the epistemic side as an issue broader than simply gathering accurate information promises to include attending to social contexts as part of responsible knowing

Addelson's account of the responsibilities of knowledge-makers differs importantly from notions of professionals serving the common good just by pursuing truth and objectivity on behalf of other community members. The point is not to abandon truth and objectivity, but to acknowledge further complexities both within disciplinary practices and in the relation of the discipline to the community. Addelson distinguishes between two conceptions of professional responsibility, one operating within the (self-regulating) discipline, and the other sensitively attuned to the creative power of professional and cognitive authority with respect to the wider society.

Her view of how knowledge is made enables Addelson to advocate a kind of professional responsibility that reflects the authority of such professionals and the different ways it can be exercised. One of Addelson's insights is that knowledge-makers can operate in a reflexive way, seeing the collective action not just as collaboration between experts, but as involving responsibilities and requiring sensitivities to those who are part of the research and to the community in general. She argues that contemporary structures of professionalism are designed to prevent such reciprocity, and that this is one of the ways that cognitive authority is maintained.[59] Here, she is pointing to conditions similar to those that would encourage or discourage virtues of epistemic justice identified by Fricker's and Rolin's virtues of civility and inclusiveness, and where invested ignorance would be likely. Professional status is often justified by service to public needs or goods. Yet "[p]rofessionals themselves have a major hand in defining the public need and good that they serve."[60] So a certain amount of bad faith or self servingness can be maintained by the profession, but I have argued against an epistemic justification for this.

These versions of epistemic responsibility and virtue involve not being blinkered by the ideal of epistemophilia to the practice of epistemic authority. They require an alternative view of knowledge because, as Addelson puts it, "[t]he individualist perspective and the old theory of knowledge, truth and science supported the authority of professionals and allowed them not only to define scientific truth but to make major contributions to the definition of how we should live."[61] This is because we look to experts to guide social policy and social change. An account of epistemic authority that simply bases authority on expertise, or access to the truth (or, according to Goldman, the capacity to answer questions in relevant domains, discussed above) both depends on and sustains a particular view of knowledge. It is a view of knowledge that renders invisible the power of epistemic authorities to define the framework and rules of knowledge, and thus to reinscribe their own authority. Competent expert practice demands knowing and taking account of one's own social position, especially if it is one of relative power and privilege, and one's authority with respect to social matters. Revising the epistemological account with ignorance in mind permits a richer account of expertise to emerge.

NOTES

1. Marilyn Frye, *The Politics of Reality: Essays in Feminist Theory* (Trumansberg, NY: The Crossing Press, 1983).

2. For an interesting discussion of authority, social delegation of authority and legitimate and illegitimate challenges to authority, see Hanrahan and Antony, "Because I Said So."

3. Rolin, "Gender and Trust," 96.

4. Rolin, "Gender and Trust," 112.

5. Rolin, "Gender and Trust," 110.

6. Jonathan E. Adler has argued that intellectual vices can have a value in an epistemic community because "[i]n real life, intellectual vices, while harmful to inquiry in some ways, are sometimes essential to its well functioning." Jonathan E. Adler, "Epistemic Dependence, Diversity of Ideas and a Value of Intellectual Vices," *The Proceedings of the Twentieth World Congress of Philosophy, Vol. III: Philosophy of Education*, ed. D. M. Steiner (Columbia: Bowling Green University Philosophical Documentation Center, 1999), 118. I agree that some vices can be valuable, but would also add that some apparent "vices" are not so vicious when we replace the univocal standard of successful inquiry (or veritism, truth-conduciveness, knowledge acquisition) with pluralistic values.

7. Political questions about who really benefits from discoveries and patterns of the division of epistemic labor are also made obscure. In chapter 4, I return to ethical and political issues related to epistemic dependence.

8. These are not necessarily the same. For example, there may be an official story on the public record, while a different account is common knowledge.

9. As discussed in the previous chapter, an explanation of how this can work is given by Audi, "The Place of Testimony," 404–22.

10. This could be problematic if the transferred knowledge is supposed to be identical for the speaker and hearer, but their contexts and relative levels of expertise are very different. P. J. Graham presents an "information-theoretic" account of this type of transfer, which would avoid such a problem: as long as the new knower has access to information, then they can be said to come to know. On Graham's analysis, the new knower need not acquire knowledge that is identical to that of the expert. P. J. Graham, "Transferring Knowledge," *NOUS* 34, no. 1 (2000): 131–52.

11. Goldman explicitly states that "Veritistic epistemology is such a special field, where the selected good is knowledge and the selected bads are error and ignorance." Goldman, *Knowledge in a Social World*, 6.

12. Goldman, "Epistemic Paternalism," 120. "Veritistic" here means related to the pursuit of truth, so he is interested in whether or not a given social practice supports or conflicts with the goal of truth.

13. Goldman, "Epistemic Paternalism," 121.

14. I am putting aside questions of first person authority, which I think are very different from questions within the division of epistemic labor.

15. See also Hanrahan and Antony, "Because I Said So." The claim that there is an important distinction between expertise and authority is not a novel one. Such a distinction is widely made, for example, in discussions of medical paternalism where expertise is uncontested, but the legitimacy and scope of the exercise of paternalistic authority is challenged.

16. A similar distinction can be found in Miranda Fricker, "Rational Authority and Social Power: Towards a Truly Social Epistemology," *Proceedings of the Aristotelian Society* 98, no. 2 (1998): 159-177. Fricker distinguishes "rational authority" which is based on trustworthiness and competence from "credibility" which refers to the features of the informant which indicate whether she or he is likely to be right about the issue in question.

17. A. L. Allen, *Uneasy Access* (Totowa, New Jersey: Rowman and Littlefield, 1988), 166.

18. Hugo A. Bedau, "Paternalism," in *The Oxford Companion to Philosophy*, ed. T. Honderich (Oxford: Oxford University Press, 1995), 647.

19. Goldman, "Epistemic Paternalism," 121.

20. Goldman, "Epistemic Paternalism," 121.

21. Contemporary debates in this area deal with "Intelligent Design" but I will stick with Goldman's focus on Creationism. I think the arguments could be applied to intelligent design.

22. Goldman, "Epistemic Paternalism," 121.

23. Those advocating that Intelligent Design ought to be taught alongside evolution often invoke "students' rights to know." This is an appeal to epistemic welfare and the perceived proper application of epistemic paternalism.

24. Sandra Harding, "Rethinking Standpoint Epistemology," in *Feminist Epistemologies*, ed. L. Alcoff and E. Potter (New York and London: Routledge, 1993), 63.

25. Goldman, "Epistemic Paternalism," 128.

26. Goldman, "Epistemic Paternalism," 131.

27. Goldman, "Epistemic Paternalism," 124.

28. Goldman, "Epistemic Paternalism," 130.

29. The difference I am trying to articulate here is similar to the difference between power seen as the direct exercise of force and a Foucauldian conception of power as a network of relations and procedures.

30. Goldman, "Epistemic Paternalism," 113 n. 2.

31. This is very similar to the position defended by Hall and Johnson (discussed in chapter 1).

32. Goldman, "Epistemic Paternalism," 113.

33. Goldman discusses the principle purported to direct the control of evidence to another (C-RTE, which I discuss further below) most carefully and thoroughly in the context of certain legal practices, specifically the rules that determine the admissibility of evidence. His discussion of law has two major problems: first, he understands the law or at least the evidence rules aspect of it as a truth seeking enterprise, and second, underlying the first error, he understands law, or this aspect of it, as rule-following. The errors in Goldman's discussion of law mean that his central case against C-RTE is not only unnecessary because C-RTE is not *prima facie* plausible, but also ineffective because his account of the main example is mistaken.

34. Goldman, "Epistemic Paternalism," 113-4.

35. Goldman, "Epistemic Paternalism," 114.

36. Goldman, "Epistemic Paternalism," 114.

37. Goldman, "Epistemic Paternalism," 114.

38. Goldman, "Epistemic Paternalism," 125.

39. Helen Longino, *The Fate of Knowledge* (Princeton and Oxford: Princeton University Press, 2002), 155.

40. S. Goonatilake, "Transfer Systems in Science and Technology and Indigenous Intellectual Initiatives," *Philosophy and Social Action* 13, no. 1–4 (1987): 15.

41. Rolin, "Gender and Trust."

42. Kathryn P. Addelson, *Moral Passages* (New York and London: Routledge, 1994), 161.

43. Addelson, *Moral Passages*, 18.

44. Addelson, *Moral Passages*, 148.

45. Vrinda Dalmiya and Linda Alcoff, "Are 'Old Wives' Tales' Justified?" in *Feminist Epistemologies*, ed. L. Alcoff and E. Potter (New York and London: Routledge, 1993), 223.

46. Dalmiya and Alcoff, "Are 'Old Wives' Tales' Justified?" 226.

47. Harding, "Rethinking Standpoint Epistemology."

48. The power to determine what counts as knowledge is a clear instance of the intersection of knowledge and power. Unlike Michel Foucault, Addelson does not analyse the power located in institutional practices. Instead, she locates responsibility in the actions of those persons who form and maintain those institutions. She is concerned with the power of professionals and intellectuals in academic institutions to determine the course of knowledge. This analysis operates at a different level from the Foucauldian analysis of the archaeology of practices and structures, because it deals with the responsibilities and virtues of epistemic agents, but the contexts are not independent as there will be mutual influence between theories and practices at both levels. See Michel Foucault, *The Archaeology of Knowledge*, trans. A. M. Sheridan Smith (New York: Routledge, 2002).

49. Rolin, "Gender and Trust," 111.

50. Sandra Harding's inclusive objectivity, Addelson's collective knowledge making, Code's analysis of epistemic responsibility and Braaten's account of intellectual virtue all point to this conclusion.

51. Linda Tuhiwai Smith provides a powerful analysis of literally imperialist knowledge. See Linda T. Smith, *Decolonizing Methodologies: Research and Indigenous Peoples* (London: Zed Books, 1999).

52. Code, *Rhetorical Spaces*, 107.

53. See Code, *Rhetorical Spaces,* 120–43.

54. When relating professionally to persons with mental illness, these are vitally important concepts. The notion of a person's capacity (to give informed consent to treatment) and the question of insight (into the nature and state of illness) are treated very differently in contemporary legislation such as the Tasmanian *Mental Health Act (1996)* from how they were understood in the past. Previous approaches presumed both a lack of capacity and need for obtaining informed consent, and little or no priority was given to the provision of clear and understandable information about diagnosis and treatment options to those receiving treatment for mental illness.

55. Julia Driver's account of the virtue of humility raises a similar issue, although she is concerned with ethical virtue and self-evaluation. Julia Driver, "The Virtues of Ignorance," *The Journal of Philosophy* 86, no. 7 (1989), 373–84. The similarity lies in the fact that the virtuous

empathizer must also avoid the vice of arrogance, and must not be too quick to presume that she knows.

56. Such discredit may be a form of oppression when the dominant cultural attitude discredits an entire social group. This would fit into the form of oppression described by Iris Young as marginalization in which "a whole category of people is expelled from useful participation in social life." Iris M. Young, *Justice and the Politics of Difference* (Princeton: Princeton University Press, 1990), 53.

57. Whipps, "Jane Addams's Social Thought as a Model for a Pragmatist-Feminist Communitarianism," *Hypatia* 10, no. 2 (2004), 127.

58. bell hooks, *Feminist Theory from Margin to Center* (Boston: South End Press, 1984), 2.

59. Addelson, *Moral Passages*, 208.

60. Addelson, *Moral Passages*, 140.

61. Addelson, *Moral Passages*, 169.

Chapter Four

Ignorance, Arrogance, and Pluralism

I have been arguing that increasing knowledge does not exhaust epistemic value, and that understanding relationships is crucial for understanding epistemic practice. Taking interdependence seriously and taking epistemic agents as members of communities yields an epistemology that intersects and even overlaps with politics and ethics. This chapter explores intersections between the epistemic account developed so far and a selection of themes from feminist epistemology, showing how an epistemology friendly to ignorance can be useful. I explore epistemic pluralism [1] looking specifically at cross cultural interactions where members of one group such as anthropologists, study another, and where scientific investigators from one community seek to learn from another's medical or botanical lore. These kinds of case show pluralism both with respect to the stories told by subjects and with respect to the irreducibility of explanations to a single unified account of phenomena. Just as epistemic virtues can refer to information or to relationships between members of an epistemic community, epistemic pluralism can focus on information or it can focus on inter-agent engagements. In the first case, pluralism arises from different theories, interpretations, or frameworks, as in scientific pluralism; in the second case, pluralism arises from different subjectivities or perspectives, for example, between members of different cultural groups. [2] The epistemic pluralism here is distinct from the value pluralism already defended. Here, the idea is that while there can be overlap and convergence between people's understandings of one another, the external world, nature, and the like, these understandings cannot be assumed to form a perfect unity, in practice or in principle. The degrees of divergence will vary, as will the contexts where one or another view can be rejected as an error, but diversity and plurality remain ineliminable aspects of the epistemic landscape.

This chapter takes a critical look at problematic forms of ignorance, in particular, invested ignorance and ignorance associated in complex ways with epistemic arrogance. I show here that while an epistemology that attends to ignorance has clear strengths, recognizing ignorance is not enough for epistemic virtue. Not all acknowledgment of one's own ignorance is constructive.

Pluralism complicates the notion of simple ignorance. What counts as knowledge (in a particular context for a particular purpose) can be contrasted not only with a lack or absence of that knowledge (simple ignorance) but other non-reducible competing accounts, descriptions, or interpretations, even within a scientific framework.[3] Achieving knowledge in a given context does not always exclude the presence of ignorance—ignorance and knowledge can, to the extent that pluralism is manifest, coexist in the same neighborhood. Taking ignorance seriously brings out this consequence of pluralism, and offers a strong reason for openness beyond and after knowledge-gain.

Any specific knowledge-related enterprise involves patterns of knowledge and ignorance. While the inquiries and practices of botanists and medical practitioners, researchers and consumers would rarely, if ever, be directly informed by the perspectives of philosophical epistemology, they represent, and even embody conceptions of knowledge and ignorance and their respective values.[4] This chapter shows how an epistemology that attends to simple ignorance can also foster attention to selective and invested ignorance and offers a critical perspective that can supplement those provided by feminist, anti-racist, and post-colonialist theorists. I acknowledge that there are important sites where ignorance is to be remedied, and show that an analysis of ignorance can be helpful in such cases. Identifying forms of ignorance helps to see not only its positive role, but also its negative sides.

Noting intersections between knowledge, privilege, and power is not new: feminist epistemologists have long been sensitive to these matters. Feminist epistemologists, social scientists and moral theorists, post-colonial, and other subaltern theorists have also paid some attention to ignorance, principally to what I term invested ignorance. Unsurprisingly, in such contexts, the downsides of ignorance are emphasized, such as the ascribed ignorance that leads to exclusion from educational and learning opportunities, and the ignorance that is part of a systematically distorted world view. These manifestations of invested ignorance have been identified in projects of knowing across racial and cultural differences, for instance, when white privileged feminists engage with issues concerning race, or when western biomedical assumptions intersect with indigenous and other groups' understandings of health and healing.

The emphasis on epistemic dependence at the heart of my analysis is indebted to feminist critiques, particularly criticisms of epistemic individualism. Like other feminist epistemologists, I acknowledge political dimensions to epistemic practices. However, my project is not initially motivated by an understanding of and opposition to gender (and other) oppressions, but by recognizing the need for an explanation and revaluation of ignorance. The revaluation of ignorance begins as a critical engagement with certain tendencies within mainstream epistemology, and the issues that arise from a serious account of epistemic interdependence converge with those that interest many feminists and other social epistemologists, specifically those of subordination and oppression between social groups. I think the arguments developed here show that epistemology on its own terms needs to take seriously considerations that feminists have raised, whether or not an explicitly feminist agenda is adopted.

While the tradition of epistemic individualism remains strong, epistemic communities and epistemic dependence (for example testimony) have become much more central and mainstream topics within epistemology, due to the work of feminist epistemologists and social epistemologists. Feminist epistemologists have often made explicit how differences in social position complicate epistemic relationships, and how attending to difference can enhance our understanding of knowledge communication.[5] Yet ignorance usually remains a state to be avoided.

I have defended a non-instrumental view of epistemic relationships in which values of recognition and participation are not reducible to knowledge-conduciveness. This emphasis on recognition, inclusion, and participation might seem redundant—we have sufficient feminist reasons to take these values and the problems of patterns of exclusion or denigration seriously— but I have shown that the neglect of ignorance and attendant lack of concern for inter-agent virtues need revision for epistemological reasons as well.

The tendency to over-value knowledge in some mainstream epistemologies obscures the need for, and even discourages a sensitivity to the kinds of "discredit" vices that can reinforce social injustices. The assumption that knowledge is good, merges into an assumption that those engaged in research, discovery, and the like are justified in their knowledge-related activities insofar as and precisely because knowledge is acquired. However, certain vicious attitudes and practices, such as arrogance and appropriation, even as they are involved in racism and sexism, have epistemic dimensions. Ways of knowing have been shown to carry sexist baggage, explicitly, in imagery[6] or in patterns of practice, precisely in the ways that some epistemic agents treat others.[7] Epistemic practices, research, data collection, and publication all have ethical, political, and legal implications and these can be compatible with or antithetical to feminist goals (perhaps most cases are mixed). These practices can also be seen in light of epistemic concerns about proper treatment of other epistemic agents. These concerns are better understood when interactions between knowledge and ignorance and their respective values are articulated carefully and critically. Acknowledging connections between epistemic and political practices and theories does not mean that politics or ethics and epistemology are perfectly aligned or coextensive—in my view, they are not. Rather, thinking about the epistemic dimension as such offers a distinctly useful perspective, as I show in this chapter.

MEDICAL PLURALISM

An ignorance friendly epistemology can contribute to understanding knowledge practices involving intercultural diversity. Medicine is a significant area of human knowledge and expertise: probably all cultures have some practices and systems for dealing with ill health. Medicine and healthcare provide rich examples of diverse understandings of illness and health and contrasting world views. The benefits of medical practice in the west depend on successful epistemic practice by both researchers and practitioners. Western biomedicine has had unsurpassed impact on cure and prevention of disease through increasing knowledge of biology, pharmacology, epidemiology, and so on. I have argued that epistemic success is not exhausted by accumulation of knowledge. By considering the pluralism of medical frameworks and different forms of medical knowledge, I will show that doing well with knowledge in many practical cases turns out to demand interpersonal epistemic virtues. The discussion will focus on health care, research, and intellectual property rights (IPR) in contexts of social diversity. Before discussing what makes for virtue and epistemic responsibility in these environments, it is worth pausing to consider the terms in which to describe some of this diversity.

Not all healthcare takes place within the framework of western scientific biomedicine. There are many traditions of healing and healthcare, and many people from western cultures use so-called "alternative" therapies.[8] Labeling is tricky in this context. Despite being labeled "alternative," such practices are not merely on the fringe of healthcare. They are a primary source of medical care in, for example, South Africa, China, and India, and among significant proportions of the population in developed countries.

It is likewise hard to decide on a label for non-western-biomedical health practices. The label "Complementary and Alternative Medicine" (CAM) places western biomedicine as the central point of reference, but "alternative" is relative to context: Chinese, Tibetan, and Ayurvedic medicine are mainstream primary healthcare forms for significant populations. A single title also belies the diversity of healthcare contexts, beliefs, and practices. Communities with healing traditions are diverse along measures of size, institutionalization of learning, effects of colonialism, and integration or compatibility with western biomedicine. The term "complementary" rightly points to how different medical systems can work together, but perhaps underestimates the potential for conflict. For example, some traditional healing ceremonies can be integrated with biomedical treatment, but those involving animal sacrifice are problematic; opposition to taking blood can conflict with common diagnostic tests; and surgery itself can be viewed as a defilement of bodily integrity.[9]

The label "indigenous" knowledge (including medical and botanical knowledge) is strained. Which groups should belong to the category, and do cultures and groups from Australia, North America, Japan, Africa, and elsewhere, really have much in common? Is Tibetan medicine indigenous knowledge? In what sense does a relocated group remain indigenous in its new locations? In addition, there are complex challenges to an outsider seeking to discuss aspects of other cultures without distortion or (direct or indirect) appropriation.[10]

Labeling knowledge as "traditional" also faces problems due in part to a presumption that "traditional" knowledge is not well founded, because it is traditional, (an attitude akin to the denigration of dependence discussed in chapter 1) and an equally problematic idealization of traditional knowledge (indigenous groups and groups like Tibetans can be over-romanticized) as more pure, genuine, or innocent than Western knowledge. Both attitudes seem to rely on a strict dichotomy between exotic and Western scientific knowledge.[11]

Grethel Aguilar contrasts Traditional Biotechnology with Modern Biotechnology.[12] Traditional Biotechnology includes agricultural and medical techniques and resources. Labeling the contrast in these terms is, however, problematic because in many contexts "[t]he sense of the word 'traditional' is that the reasons or explanations most commonly produced by such thought systems are little more than an appeal *to* tradition."[13] This connotation is recognized as pejorative, implying an unenlightened attitude to knowing that lacks critical reflection (perhaps succumbing to dogmatism). Due to this negative connotation, contrasting scientific knowledge with traditional knowledge likely makes the latter appear inferior. Specifying "technology" as Aguilar does, goes some way to alleviating this concern because that label emphasizes development and deliberate cultivation. In addition, inheriting the knowledge of a tradition is not necessarily a passive participation, and many aspects of western academic study can be seen as participation in a tradition. In any case, people in all cultures succumb to uncritical reliance on tradition at times (Kant points this out, calling it "immaturity"[14]) so the presence of passive or uncritical dependence does not distinguish some kinds of culture from others. In line with my defence of epistemic dependence, I advocate a positive conception of tradition, which includes respect, acknowledgement and engagement, and which can apply to western biomedical practices. Thus Modern Biotechnology is "modern" not due to lacking tradition and interdependence, but because of an emphasis on particular understandings of discovery, scientific standards, and progress.

In spite of these qualifications and caveats, I will refer to traditional and to indigenous knowledge for want of better terms in which to present some contrasts with western scientific knowledge. The pluralism evident in this area includes similarity as well as contrast, convergence as well as tension. This permits the ambivalence with which traditional expertise can be treated: local experts must know about medicinal properties if bioprospecting can make any sense, yet for the purposes of proper credit and compensation, they seem not to be recognized as knowers. This slippage is enabled by an uncritical view of knowledge collection, and an epistemologically and morally suspect view of whose understanding really counts as knowledge.

Contrasting models of knowledge are evident in various discussions of knowledge of nature and medicine. Frédérique Apffel-Marglin discussing Andean "Traditional Biotechnology" (not her phrase) cites the use of metaphors of conversation and nurturing,[15] referring to the mutual connections between indigenous knowers in the Andes and their environment.[16] She reports a description of the relationship between Andean cultivators and their crops and environment in this way: "We have great faith in what nature transmits to us. These indicators are not the result of the science of humans nor either the invention of people with great experience. Rather, it is the voice of nature itself which announces to us the manner in which we must plant our crops."[17]

As Apffel-Marglin argues, knowledge and land are part of the culture that unites the group. The knowledge of such farmers is clearly not, in their own view, detached from and independent of the land and its produce. The environment does not merely furnish evidence, but is rather acknowledged as an informant, an "announcer," a trusted expert. Neither information nor crops are seen just as resources to be used for maximum benefit. From the side of interpersonal epistemic virtues, epistemic agents are seen in light of an epistemic well-being that is not reducible to quantities of information, and in light of social arrangements in which credibility and authority are negotiated. Nature itself communicates as an epistemic agent.

Although there is a great deal of diversity among them, healing practices outside western biomedicine often emphasize holism. Lori Arviso Alvord, the first Navajo woman surgeon, describes a Navajo healer's approach in implicit contrast to the biomedical approach in which she has been trained: "A *haatatii* did not treat a person's liver or spleen or appendix—although, as in the case of Dezgah Tsosie, they could be perfectly aware that a problem resided in such an organ. But they did not isolate a part from the whole. Their medicine was for the whole human creature—body, mind and spirit, their community, and even the larger world."[18]

In a holistic view, a sufferer is seen as a person whose embodied condition might reflect psychic, social, *and* biological attributes. People have not only internal mental characteristics but also inhabit a spiritual and/or emotional social environment such that other entities can cause illness. For example, the ill will of a living person or a spirit can cause illness, and remedies must respond to such.

Approaches to healing show up differently from the perspective of knowledge collection, in contrast to interpersonal epistemic virtues. From the perspective of knowledge collection, one is doing well as a knower if one acquires and shares new and useful information. The herbal knowledge of healers in various cultural traditions is seen as a resource that can be used to increase human knowledge and to relieve human suffering through development of scientifically proven medicines and hence worth acquiring and using. Holism and connections between knowledge and its contexts tend to drop out of knowledge collection practices—the testable "active ingredient" is sought, subjected to testing, purified and made into a manufacturable remedy to be marketed.

An epistemological account that recognizes the heterogeneity of knowledge, the importance of engagement, and the multiplicity of epistemic perspectives lends itself to the holistic view of healthcare that is often seen as characteristic of non-western healing systems, in contrast to the biomedical tendency to see just a physical condition, not a whole person. However, here too, there are overlaps between these approaches. For example, within holistic practices physical interventions can be precisely targeted (as in the use of herbs to induce abortion) and conversely, biomedical practice can recognize "whole person" considerations as when grief or stress affect health; increased attention to cultural issues and "lifestyle factors." Furthermore, individuals with affiliations to more than one tradition find ways to integrate their practices. Nevertheless, a purely symptomatic treatment is more pervasive in western biomedicine than other healing traditions. This focus on symptoms detached from a person's whole context parallels the epistemic collector view of information as detachable from systems of understanding and from persons who know.

Because of the holistic perspective of many healers, the natural world is related in more complex ways to an individual's and a community's well being than merely as a resource for finding ways to treat symptoms. Alvord offers the example of an initially inexplicable illness affecting a Navajo community recognized by Medicine Men as caused by "disturbed natural patterns in the universe"[19] specifically "an excess of rainfall which had caused the piñon trees to bear too much fruit."[20] Ultimately, the Center for Disease Control identified a hantavirus spread by deer mice whose population had exploded due to the increased piñon crop. In Alvord's words: "Many generations ago, astonishingly, the keen observational skills of Navajo peo-

ple and their harmony with the natural world had led them to observe relationships with the environment and animal world that had, in the end, helped
the CDC narrow their search to the mouse. Our ancestors were astute epi-
demiologists."[21]

Herbal and local remedies are not seen as something to remove, refine,
test, and form into drugs, but rather as embedded in complex relations and
interactions. The tendency to abstract symptoms from overall health in western biomedical systems is compounded by the embeddedness of healthcare
practice in systems of delivery of products and services that are clearly
quantified and costed, within capitalistic economies. Global pharmacological
companies and massive management systems for health care delivery push
towards precise uniform symptom-based treatments that tend to be abstracted
from the messy complexities of a person's whole well being. Economies of
scale require some kinds of uniformities of treatments. Evidence-based medicine takes accumulated data, necessarily abstracted from patient's lives as the
foundation for clinical decision-making.[22]

This is not to say that such uniformity is all bad—clear and precise
protocols are desirable and effective in many circumstances. And public
health can benefit from uniform access to some services and products—for
example, treatment for malaria, infant diarrhea, and so on. Furthermore, as
Julie Stone has argued, "[e]very health-care relationship gives rise to ethical
issues, even if the therapy itself is relatively innocuous."[23] Western biomedicine has strict requirements of professional codes of ethics, professional development, and complaints management and while these are not perfect,
these safeguards are sometimes absent from other healthcare provision systems. Western medical practice has its strengths.

The epistemophilic views here contested hold that the sole epistemic
value is roughly holding true beliefs or knowledge, and that acquiring such
beliefs in some reliable fashion (and sometimes also sharing them) exhausts
an agent's epistemic obligations. On such views, there is nothing epistemically problematic about acquiring botanical and herbal information from local herbalists and making it more widely available through scientific processes of checking, publishing, etc. I want to suggest this might not be so, and
that some ways of collecting and disseminating information are *epistemically*
irresponsible. In other words, there are epistemic as well as moral and political issues associated with practices known as bio-prospecting and bio-piracy
such as the instrumental treatment of other knowers, failure to fully recognize epistemic authority and the like. These are not reducible to mere veritistic consequences of the practices, or whether or not true beliefs are acquired
or disseminated, even indirectly by looking at what might impede or encourage cooperation between members of diverse communities. Rather, the point
is that epistemic responsibility demands recognizing the relationship between
a course of action and past events, such as actions of colonialization, dismis-

sal or appropriation, and the ways that invested ignorance might obscure this recognition.

Intellectual property rights are more often based on the ways of understanding knowledge that I have argued are problematic: some aspects of justifications for intellectual property rights in the Western institution of intellectual property display epistemophilia—an excessive enthusiasm for knowledge as the only epistemic good—and a pure instrumentalism—a system is favored insofar as it looks to be an effective method of increasing knowledge.

> Granting property rights to producers is here seen as necessary to ensure that enough intellectual products (and the countless other goods based on these products) are available to users. . . . This approach . . . establishes a right to restrict the current availability and use of intellectual products for the purpose of increasing the production and thus future availability and use of new intellectual products.[24]

Hettinger's analysis explicitly cites increased intellectual production as the purpose that justifies intellectual property rights. Thus it suits Modern Biotechnological practitioners better than Traditional Biotechnological practitioners, unsurprisingly as the moderns do precisely what it is designed to encourage. This is not the only way to conceive of intellectual property, and the protection of commercial interests and maximization of knowledge are not the only relevant considerations. We can benefit in an epistemic sense from a proper appreciation of different forms of knowledge, from being clear about epistemic responsibilities, and from recognizing and promoting the virtues that contribute to our being good knowers in a resilient epistemic community. (Intellectual property is only one area of regulated epistemic practice that could be enhanced by attention to epistemic virtues; others include informed consent and freedom of information.) Rather than regarding knowledge as a neutral object with no connections to persons, knowledge should be understood in a way that reflects relationships between knowers, and virtues of engagement. If I am responsible and epistemically virtuous, I should ask how that knower understands the information, rather than treating it as atomistically detachable from the knower and the community, or presuming that their perspective on its permissible use coincides with mine. I should see my actions as forming part of a relationship between knowers, in which I have responsibilities, rather than as a mere exercise in finding information. I ought to think about what this knower wants to teach me, not just about what information I think it would be useful to acquire. I should consider trust and trustworthiness, both as part of my own practice, and as attributes that might be understood differently by knowers from a different community. I ought to think about confidentiality and disclosure, and the possibility that these are understood differently. In general, I should think about my interactions as contributing to relationships with the knower with whom I am conversing. Am I treating every knower I encounter as evidence, or have I made epistemic commitments to trust, and have I lived up to those who trust me? Fundamentally, am I treating other knowers with respect, or merely as an instrument for my own epistemic ends? Self-reflective consideration of both simple and invested ignorance will deliver a different assessment of epistemic practices than a consideration of rights or knowledge-maximizing. This is not merely a consideration of fairness and justice, although improper denial of others' knowledge can be an injustice. It is, additionally, a way of responding to the diversity within my epistemic community, and the different positions and perspectives of knowers with whom I interact, and our various and more or less problematic patterns of ignorance and knowledge.

To a significant extent, an understanding of knowledge defines and determines what is protected by intellectual property regulation. The fundamental mistake of seeing knowledge and ignorance as antithetical and knowledge as always good (hence the goodness of acquiring it), coupled with a narrow scientific discovery-based model of knowledge can coincide with the unjust practices Joseph Githaiga criticizes in the following remarks: "There is, therefore, a clear bias in the operation of these laws in favor of the pharmaceutical industry and other institutions based in the industrialized nations. The modern patent laws allow these institutions to monopolize the benefits derived from the exploitation of indigenous knowledge at the expense of indigenous people's interests."[25]

My aim is to focus not on economic exploitation, or the justice or otherwise of distribution of benefits from pharmaceutical development, but on what views of knowledge show up in these practices and regulations.

Grethel Aguilar points to the epistemic dimensions of intellectual property rights (IPR) debates: "At the moment [in 2001], the IPR systems are not appropriate for protection of traditional knowledge because they cannot fully respond to the characteristics of certain forms of traditional knowledge like collective ownership, oral transmission, public domain (some cases) communal origination, collective management, and ownership of information and knowledge."[26] The practice of sourcing knowledge of traditional remedies from indigenous peoples is associated with substantial profits for pharmaceutical or agribusiness companies and has been described as bio-prospecting, or bio-piracy[27] because the financial benefits of new cultivated plant varieties and new medical technologies tend not to accrue to indigenous peoples who, in addition, are generally last in line for healthcare improvements.

The legal status of intellectual property rights over life-forms is controversial (for example, consider India's long battle in US and EU courts over an attempt to patent Neem by agro-chemical company W. R. Grace). There are extensive legal conflicts about transference of property rights between and competing interests of those with Traditional Biotechnological knowledge and groups or corporations with Modern Biotechnological knowledge. Patenting agreements have taken place between states and corporations, sometimes without acknowledgement of indigenous groups.[28] India, Peru, and Brazil have spearheaded efforts to "amend World Trade Organization rules [administering the Agreement of Trade Related Aspects of Intellectual Property Rights (TRIPS)] to require patent holders to disclose the origin of their patents and share benefits when those patents are based on genetic plant material or traditional knowledge from developing countries."[29] Biotech firms including Merck, Pfizer, Procter & Gamble, and General Electric have formed the American Bioindustry Alliance for ongoing opposition to such amendments.[30] It has been argued with respect to ownership and patenting of genetic materials that "[t]here is a striking asymmetry inherent in the relationship between, on the one hand, the indigenous groups and local communities, and on the other hand, the groups acquiring the information, such as multinational pharmaceutical companies."[31] The pattern of epistemic interaction that reflects and reinforces this power asymmetry involves the treatment of indigenous knowers as instruments and sources of knowledge, but not as fully fledged epistemic agents with whom corporations must engage responsibly. Within the system, there are divisions of labor such that some individuals learn from indigenous people, some work in laboratories, some manage the corporate legal approach and so on. Thus the epistemic interaction is not just the face to face encounter between a western botanical collector and a local expert, but the whole system up to and including international laws and conventions.

The development of medicines (from traditional herbs or otherwise) is a scientific practice that is said both to advance human knowledge, and to promote human welfare. When ideals such as advancing human knowledge and the good of humankind are invoked, it is important to look closely at what kinds of knowledge are being considered legitimate and what kinds of consideration affect knowledge acquisition. A simple presumption that knowledge is good tends to obscure the specific account of knowledge that operates in any given context. Any specific understanding of knowledge, or use of a particular model of knowledge, can produce different patterns of what counts as known or unknown, who counts as knowledgeable, who is credited with knowledge, and who counts as ignorant. Furthermore, the presumed goodness of knowledge tends to focus on accumulating information, to the neglect of a broader range of epistemic virtues. As I have argued, epistemic responsibility is not limited to collecting and checking facts and evidence, and the treatment of other knowers merely as sources or instruments of knowledge can indicate a lack of epistemic virtue even in cases of increasing knowledge.

According to standard epistemological accounts, agents interested in knowledge are interested in acquiring it, and/or increasing it within or for their community. But taking epistemic interdependence seriously requires further dimensions of epistemic responsibility to be recognized. In many, even most, cases of acquiring knowledge, it matters how and from whom it is obtained; many people remember particular teachers more than particular facts. In many, even most, cases of transmitting knowledge, it matters who we are telling; knowers are discreet, selective and sensitive deliverers of information. These qualities, not indiscrimination, are the epistemic norms for persons in a community of knowers, and attention to the relationships between knowers ought also to be a priority for scientific knowers engaging with indigenous knowers and to the regulation of knowledge through intellectual property institutions.

Knowledge-collector and knowledge-maximizing models are reflected in a way of doing science that aspires to an ideal of omniscience, an ideal of complete and gapless knowledge. This approach suggests that knowledge is implicitly taken to be like a jigsaw puzzle where we seek the missing pieces that supplement and reinforce the existing structure, forming a unified whole. Such an image also implies that the "world of facts" is "out there" (the truth is out there), its elements awaiting discovery, a unitary rather than a pluralistic view of knowledge. Then, these facts or evidence, treated properly—that is, checked, tested, and properly positioned within a scientific system—become legitimate knowledge. The puzzle metaphor is limited in application as patterns can be revised as with a Kuhnian paradigm shift, and new areas can be opened up by new fields of inquiry. But I think all these kinds of scientific practice can coexist with an implicit view of the progress of knowledge toward completion. The "discovery" model suits some scientific activities, and the corporations who profit from them.[32] But this model aligns with the spectator-collector model of epistemic activity, in which knowledge acquired through epistemic dependence is treated in a limited way, so that people cooperate only as sources and instruments, and even when they can be informants in Craig's sense, some aspects of epistemic participation such as full credit and acknowledgement are neglected.

As I have argued earlier, in knowing through testimony and trust, we know through complex forms of epistemic dependence, not only through collection and transmission. The extended model suggests that rewards for scientific effort ought to be part of a system that recognizes engagement and interdependence as well as discovery or novelty. The currently recognized epistemic reasons—increasing knowledge—are too narrow. Furthermore, the range of epistemic virtues agents require demand acknowledgement of complex dimensions of agency and community, not just abilities to collect information.

Much discussion of ideas like epistemic injustice emerges within feminist philosophy. In the words of Jane Duran, feminist epistemologies have at their heart "the core concerns of recognition of the other, the other's personhood, and the other's status as speaker."[33] Further, they have a concern with social patterns in which one gender is subordinated to another, with regards to recognition, personhood, and status. (This concern need not and probably cannot exclude concern for other oppressive social patterns.) On my analysis, epistemic injustice is not limited to unfair deprivation of knowledge, but includes discredit, so is not reducible to a veritistic loss, although such a loss might well be involved. Such discredit often follows social patterns, but need not do so. (For example, a dismissal of mainstream expert views on health by advocates of some alternative therapies could involve discredit or a lack of credence, but would not necessarily follow lines of social privilege and disadvantage.) Epistemic injustice shows up vividly within epistemology when the exclusive value of knowledge conduciveness is abandoned.[34]

Here, my suggestion is that the epistemophilic framework which mandates collecting and transmitting knowledge implies a right as well as a responsibility to conduct such epistemic practices and thus, tends towards a colonialist and appropriative attitude to inquiry and knowledge acquisition. This attitude is notoriously problematic from a range of subaltern perspectives. Importantly it aligns not only with other forms of colonialist practice, but also with the standard view within analytic epistemology. If we think about intersections of knowledge in the case of indigenous and biomedical understandings of health and healing, it is clear biomedical practice standardly operates in line with a knowledge collection view—things have to be evidence based, consistent with what is already known, and compatible with an accumulative or progressive model. The important achievements of this approach to medicine are undeniable and the point of the above discussion is not to disparage the achievements of biomedicine and science. Rather it is to show first that a problematic philosophical view of knowledge has real world resonance, and second that a pluralistic and non-epistemophilic view of epistemic value can be constructively applied to areas of intellectual property rights, health, medicine, and healing.

While epistemic virtue and the right view of epistemic responsibility can contribute to addressing social injustices, they will not suffice for eliminating problematic attitudes. For example, Jane Addams worked to enact a "feminist-pragmatism" in Hull House, intended to permit "reciprocal assistance—the upper-class educated women and the working class industrial workers would learn from each other, hopefully alleviating some of their handicaps through interaction."[35] Theoretical or academic views could there be developed or amended through proximity and collaboration with practice and experience, and Hull House also brought together resources for culture, arts, and education as well as energy and activism for social progressive projects. The project was designed for mutual respect between diverse parties, and exchanges of information were not the primary focus. In Addams' approach to knowledge, arrogance and epistemophilia are both avoided. People learn across diversity, but not as arrogant collectors or deliverers of knowledge. Others are not mere sources or instruments of information, but participants in their own right. Yet Shannon Sullivan has noted residual racism and classism in Jane Addams: "However, one can simultaneously recognize and attempt to offset unequal power between parties by creating a situation in which both fully participate, and leave in place racist assumptions or stereotypes about the parties involved."[36] A revised epistemology can help to identify and address social injustices, but no single strategy will eliminate them.

Acknowledging room for valuable ignorance within an epistemological framework does not mean that ignorance is always benign. The next section explores the limits of valuable ignorance.

ARROGANCE AND PROBLEMATIC IGNORANCE

There is a clear need to understand invested ignorance as part of responding to and contesting social injustice and privilege. Discussing (white feminists' and her own) efforts to contend with white privilege, Marilyn Frye points out that "[w]hile one is educating oneself about the experiences and perspectives of the peoples one is ignorant about, and in part as a corrective to the errors of one's ways, one should also be studying one's own ignorance."[37] The ignorance here is implicitly identified as part of entrenched racism, and presumably one studies one's ignorance in order to remedy it. Here Frye makes it clear that failure to recognize and know about unjust and oppressive practices allows them to continue unchecked. Our knowledge of social hierarchies and of other groups is lacking in many cases because our justifications are self-serving, our reasoning distorted, our observation inaccurate, our access restricted, our advice faulty, and the like. Ignorance of privilege itself serves to entrench and hide privilege.

Along similar lines, Charles Mills points to an "epistemological contract" embedded within the racial contract.[38] Here, ignorance is not a mere absence of knowledge, but part of a systematic ordering of what "everybody" knows and takes for granted, of who counts as credible about which matters, about sources of authority and so on. Lorraine Code argues that "[s]ocial, sexual, racial contracts require, construct, and condone an epistemology" in which ignorance, error and misinterpretation are fundamental.[39] This is why Frye rightly insists on studying one's own ignorance—the aim is not just to add the information (about other peoples or social conditions) that was lacking (remedying simple ignorance), but to understand the patterns that have established and continue to maintain epistemic and other privileges and how one's own life and social position figure in those patterns (addressing invested ignorance).

These harmful forms of invested ignorance are undeniably important. But since the negative roles of ignorance are already well-established, I have not taken an extensive discussion of problematic ignorance to be a priority for this book. My arguments are meant to establish that there is no blanket epistemic imperative to remedy ignorance, but it remains the case that ignorance should be remedied when there are good (local) reasons for doing so. Crucially, although harmful in many situations, not all ignorance is of the kind that supports the oppressive structures that feminists and others oppose. In fact, the ignorance of a dominant group can be used for resistant activities. Marilyn Frye for instance gives an example where a slave's communications leading to a successful escape are overlooked precisely because the writer who is interviewing her does not realize that as she hums and sings she is conspiring with other slaves.[40] But this strategic use of ignorance does not exhaust its value.[41]

In some cases, knowledge acquisition and transmission can be oppressive. Appropriative knowledge was discussed in relation to empathy where I showed that recognizing a space of ignorance that is *not* for me to fill with knowledge is intrinsically part of responsible empathy. But appropriation and arrogance are not limited to empathic contexts. Treating members of certain social groups merely as instruments for acquiring knowledge or as objects to be known has been part of some interactions between ethnologists, linguists, and anthropologists and "exotic" others.[42] People are told about their language, traditions, and history by scholarly experts, and sometimes the ways of telling, the presumed authority to tell, and the very categories that order the information emerge from and converge with colonialism and racism. The perfect oracular transmission of information between Dennis and Christopher discussed in chapter 1 looks even more distant from reality if we imagine one to be an expert anthropologist and the other to be a member of an indigenous group. Thinking about ignorance in a range of ways, not merely as a state best remedied, helps to develop a non-oppressive epistemology that can be sensitive to "world-view" pluralism.

Arrogance as an epistemic vice is antithetical to such pluralism. Some appropriative and transmissive practices are manifestations of arrogance, a moral vice with both moral/political and epistemic dimensions. Its epistemic side can involve ignorance or knowledge: both can be defended by an arrogant attitude. Arrogance is, among other things, an impediment to critical self-assessment. The kind of account of ignorance developed here can go some way to off-setting that impediment because an automatic positive evaluation of knowledge (or knowledge-conducive traits) is not available. More subtle and textured evaluative considerations are required.

I show here that arrogant practices are problematic from the epistemic side as well as vulnerable to political or moral criticism. I argue that the neglect of ignorance in those accounts that endorse a spectator-collector model of epistemic agency tend to generate unsatisfactory and unsustainable accounts of knowing along with a view of knowledge that excludes (or at least discourages) attention to social differences. But attention to ignorance is not always a remedy: ignorance, too, can be treated arrogantly and uncritically. Arrogance is a central epistemic vice that does not co-vary with knowledge and ignorance. Epistemic arrogance can be manifest in a smug self-satisfied approach to collecting or presenting knowledge, just as ignorance can support an arrogant attitude to others. That both ignorance and knowledge can support arrogance, complicity, and various forms of supremacy suggests that neither ignorance nor knowledge can be presumed good. Both can be arrogant or can mediate arrogance.

Feminist philosophers such as María Lugones, Marilyn Frye, and Lorraine Code have noted the importance of arrogance. Robin Dillon's account of arrogance suggests that it "typically involves more than one's already illegitimate share of power, rights, and authority."[43] This makes sense in epistemic contexts, where an arrogant agent can over-claim authority by dogmatism, dismissing challenges, ignoring alternative views or requests for justification or discrediting another epistemic agent's claims. A division of epistemic labor which defines experts according to their (our) authority and expertise can be an invitation to this kind of arrogance.

Dillon's suggestion that arrogance aligns with power and with an illegitimate disregard of others has a clear epistemic correlate. Patterns of epistemic paternalism and of subordination fit this notion of arrogance, since it is from a position of privilege and greater (illegitimate) share of authority that arrogance is manifest. Epistemic arrogance is a trap for intellectuals and experts, and as the history of academic feminism in the twentieth century shows, well intentioned women of white privilege and intellectual success can unwittingly succumb to this arrogance.[44]

A critical attitude to both knowledge and ignorance can help to counter epistemic arrogance. A critical attitude to ignorance does not mean always to remedy it; a critical attitude to knowledge does not mean always to increase it. An undiscriminating attitude to knowledge is less common in practice than theory—perhaps because it is patently unworkable—but nevertheless, an assumption that knowledge is valuable is rarely questioned. I think that the discrimination that characterizes knowledge practices suggests that the value of knowledge is contextual, provisional, and variable to the extent that knowledge can have epistemic disvalue, and epistemology does well to follow practice in this regard.

Virtues opposed to the vice of epistemic arrogance are virtues of respect for other epistemic agents understood as more than sources or instruments of knowledge. They form a cluster including Rolin's norms of civility; those of self and social awareness concerning social position and status and their effects on credibility, as discussed by Fricker; and those required for imaginative and critical evaluation of an epistemic community, including Jane Braaten's feminist intellectual virtues and those related to empathy and humility in both intimate and institutional or professional settings. This cluster replaces an unqualified desire for increasing knowledge, an attachment to what is known, and an inability to recognize that even successful collection and acquisition of knowledge can have epistemic costs, with a critical attitude to both knowledge and ignorance. This critical attitude extends to both information (which may be forgone, withheld or limited), to one's own achievements and dispositions, and to other agents whose contributions to epistemic community are not limited to knowledge acquisition and provision or production. The epistemophilic over-attachment to what is or can be known, and tendency to insist on or exaggerate its value can also yield an arrogant dogmatism, but the relationships between arrogance and ignorance are complicated.

Arrogant perception in Marilyn Frye's terms involves an intractable and dogmatic view of the world such that resistance or contestations reveal that their proponents are wrong or misguided. Dogmatism is a recognized vice on mainstream epistemic accounts.[45] Dogmatism is independent of epistemophilia, but they can be mutually reinforcing: one can be dogmatic about the exclusive value of knowledge, or one's commitment to the importance and value of knowledge can obscure the dogmatic way one shares or acquires information. Less obviously vicious (from a mainstream epistemic perspective) is thinking one is entitled to acquire knowledge from others, since on many accounts, there is a standing obligation to acquire and/or contribute to others' knowledge.[46]

Arrogance does not arise only across political difference. María Lugones ascribes arrogance to herself—in contrast to "loving perception"—and in this case, the arrogance is not displayed across a hierarchy of social groups, but from a daughter to her mother. Attention to epistemic responsibility can offset the tendency to arrogance in both political and intimate contexts. Lugones recommends "disloyalty to arrogant perceivers, including the arrogant perceiver in ourselves."[47] To know other persons, a "loving perception" that recognizes more than information increase as well as more than accurate observation is required.

Not all endorsements of ignorance are positive. Arrogance can be manifest in willful ignorance. Lorraine Code discusses James Mill's acknowledgement (and endorsement) of his own ignorance.[48] As Mill produces his *History of India*, he takes his ignorance of Indian languages and cultures to provide the ground for an objective history of that country. While I think ignorance *can* facilitate knowledge (in double blind drug tests, for example), in this case, Mill is self-deceived and mistaken. He is self-consciously aware of his ignorance, taking it as a prerequisite for an objective account, but he does not know better for failing to gain access to Indian languages and cultural products. In this case, ignorance functions to condone the view of a *terra nullius* open for colonial exploitation and "civilization" by representatives of the British Empire. As Code points out, "This manifest arrogance at the basis of Mill's judgments of India seems plainly to count both as epistemically irresponsible and immoral, for arrogance qualifies, on many accounts, as a morally reprehensible stance."[49] Mill shows himself to be arrogant about his capacity to acquire knowledge independently. Clearly Mill's attitude to his ignorance is problematic and contrary to his self-assessment; ignorance impedes rather than enhances his own project. His ignorance is pernicious, despite his awareness of it, and his arrogance constitutes epistemic as well as moral vice.

It might seem that for Mill to conduct his historical project responsibly and virtuously, his ignorance needs to be dispelled on at least two fronts. Not only does he need to know about India, he needs to know his need to know. (He perhaps needs further to know about colonialist injustices in order to avoid complicity in them, though this knowledge is not as easily accessible to him as it would be to a contemporary writer.) If Mill is to find out about India, he must depend on local informants, those who know the languages and cultures. Here, judicious recognition of his own ignorance, both invested and simple, both aspects that can be remedied and aspects that cannot, and of the virtues of epistemic dependence (not limited to transmission capacities) will help to avoid the arrogant vices leading to epistemic appropriation and arrogant perception. A responsible epistemic agent undertaking a historical project like Mill's would need some or all of the characteristics, which are well-articulated in standard accounts of epistemic virtue—open-mindedness, intellectual sobriety, proportioning belief to evidence and courage—virtues that would also be useful for a scientist proposing and testing hypotheses.[50] These are standard virtues of autonomous inquiry and investigation—the virtues of the pursuit of knowledge. An epistemically virtuous historian would also need selectivity and discrimination, capacities to sort relevant from irrelevant detail, and to see significant connections as well as coincidences. A historian would also need to supplement these characteristics with a respect for others as more than sources or instruments, a capacity for both the trust and reliance forms of epistemic dependence and a sense of when each is appropriate; and a capacity to implement Rolin's norms of civility. Further, an agent might need some awareness of the effects of position and status on credibility, displayed as the virtues of epistemic justice described by Fricker, and as the empathic capacities explained in chapter 3. A critically responsible historian might also benefit from Braaten's feminist intellectual virtues, enabling critical evaluation of one's own epistemic community, as well as one's own attitudes. Perhaps either individual attention to or collective concern about inclusion would enable members of the community being studied to be participant knowledge makers. (According to Kathryn Addelson, diversifying the community of knowledge makers entails that the game itself is open for revision. For her, the idea of inclusion means more than offering the possibility of joining our game on our terms and in line with the rules already established.[51])

The distinction between positive and negative presences of ignorance is not that between active and passive or self-aware and oblivious ignorance. A positive form of ignorance is involved in humility, and in valuing others' discrimination and discretion rather than just the opportunity to acquire their information and reciprocally to transmit one's own. Dealing with ignorance is part of dealing with information that is inevitably partial, and of acknowledging perspectival aspects of knowledge. James Mill's ignorance is quite different. Mill concedes his own knowledge of India is incomplete and limited, but his attitude to this selectivity and to his own perspective is arrogant in assuming that nation can offer him nothing that would improve his ability to write a knowledgeable history.

Certain social institutions discourage critical insight as they encourage arrogant perception and pernicious ignorance. A person may live, as did George Eliot's Gwendolen Harlech, according to Lorraine Code, embedded in an "instituted social imaginary" from which it is extremely difficult to know better, or at least easy to remain oblivious to various aspects of social arrangements.[52] Until her family suffers a reverse in fortunes, Harlech lives in "leisured affluence" in which she is "oblivious to her own class position and its privilege."[53] As Code points out, socially privileged ignorance might be in need of remedy, but is not always culpable. Harlech's ignorance may not be entirely her own fault, since like other women of her class and time, she is surrounded by significant explicit and tacit impediments and disincentives that count against her becoming better informed. It would take extraordinary efforts and it would attract severe social disapprobation were she to try to learn about and examine critically her own society's institutions. These very institutions keep women like her "in ignorance by depriving them of everything that might nourish their intelligence."[54] If Gwendolyn Harlech and others like her are not culpable, it is in part because of the (paternalistic) structures that shelter them, but simultaneously prevent them from knowing very much. Nevertheless, such ignorance of their social context is regrettable not merely because of that deprivation, but because when shared by many members of a dominant or privileged class, it aligns with and facilitates those social structures of dominance and subordination that feminists oppose. It becomes, or reinforces invested ignorance, as well as, in the case of women, being a form of subordination. We could call this subordinating aspect "exclusionary ignorance," as real or presumed ignorance is used to keep certain individuals or members of some groups from full participation in epistemic interactions. Gwendolyn Harlech exemplifies both complicit (arguably non-culpable) and exclusionary ignorance and her case suggests that exclusionary

and invested ignorance can reinforce one another. Harlech is both subordinated by and privileged by patterns of ignorance.

George Eliot does not present Harlech purely as an innocent victim of a
society that facilitates ignorance in women of a certain class. In fact, Harlech
shows little concern for others, and is presented initially as selfish and self
centered, concerned mainly with being admired, and thinking little of others.
Arguably, she suffers from an epistemic arrogance as well as ignorance. (Her
later efforts to improve are hampered by her lack of resources, both internal
and in her environment.) Eliot herself was unconventional and socially
aware, and *Daniel Deronda* reflects this in its sympathetic portrayal of the
individual characters, of social prejudices and how people overcome them.
But the contrast between the options available to the characters of Gwendolyn Harlech and Daniel Deronda indicates the way that gendered social ordering inhibits women's development.

The convergences of knowledge and power, ignorance and subordination,
and ignorance and entrenched privilege in these examples provide a *prima
facie* case for the importance of overcoming ignorance. Because ignorance
often reinforces or permits oppressive relations, it is generally seen negatively from an ethical or political perspective. And there are good reasons for
this. Ignorance, real or ascribed, can have damaging and pernicious effects. A
person, however well intentioned, may be ignorant in ways that allow her
beliefs and conduct to align with and uphold patterns of social injustice
although this complicit ignorance will have varying degrees of culpability.
An individual who is deprived of information or knowledge is highly vulnerable to control, manipulation and error, and being deemed ignorant can be
disempowering as well as insulting.

Prescriptions, manifestations, or ascriptions of ignorance are common
ingredients of subordination and oppression. They establish patterns that
underpin some specifically *epistemic* forms of injustice, like the discredit
suffered by Marge Sherwood, discussed in chapter 2.[55] Marge Sherwood
arguably does not suffer as did Gwendolyn Harlech from a deprivation of
information, nor from the flaw of self obsession nor the vice of arrogance—
she knows well enough that Ripley has somehow dealt with her fiancé. But
she is deemed ignorant, so suffers exclusion from or restrictions within the
epistemic community such that she cannot be an authoritative source for
Ripley senior and the detective Macarron. Rolin's norms of civility can be
applied to such informal cases. "A normatively adequate theory of scientific
testimony must address not only the question of what constitutes trustworthy
character, but also the question of what properties are reliable indicators of
trustworthiness."[56] Likewise, in non-scientific contexts, we need to check
that recognition of trustworthiness is on the basis of properties that are not
differentially attributed on the basis of social privilege. Here again we see the

significance of feminist arguments that gender ideologies and stereotypes construct how people are divergently perceived as credible.

Yet people can be arrogant about the knowledge ascribed to others as well as about ascribed ignorance. Some forms of colonialist appropriation involve the acquisition of knowledge (or reduction of ignorance), when members of a privileged group take themselves to have an entitlement to know about another culture. Mill's arrogance is manifest in his failure to see that he has any thing to learn from the Indian people about whose nation he wants to write a history. Andrea Smith has pointed to a different manifestation of arrogance when discussing new age uptake (appropriation) of Native American spirituality. She reports Indian (Native American) women being "told we are greedy if we do not choose to share our spirituality" and sees this demand for information and insistence on inclusion as a practice that promotes "the subordination of Indian women to white women."[57] The attitude of entitlement positions Indian women at the service of non-indigenous women, such that the desires of the privileged take precedence over Indian women's priorities.

A similar sense of entitlement when present in experts who study other groups like ethnographers, linguists, and anthropologists is sometimes a vicious consequence of an enthusiasm for knowledge collection. There are notorious medical experiments that treat other persons merely as objects of study. With the best will in the world, academics, and experts sometimes assume both an entitlement to know about and acquire information from others, and that when they tell others how it is, they are sharing their hard won knowledge as a gift and it should be appreciated as such. This is at times epistemically arrogant, and the epistemic vices often (though not always) converge with racist or sexist attitudes. A narrow understanding of epistemic responsibility and an excessive commitment to the value of knowledge increase could lead an agent to seek and share information in arrogant ways even while she is committed to anti-oppressive politics. In such a case, the problem might be not that theory and practice are misaligned, but instead that practice is consistent with a mistaken view informed by (probably tacit) epistemic theory. The benefits of taking ignorance seriously can also be seen in cases from science and medicine. An epistemology that includes critical attention to ignorance offers resources to consider issues of epistemic justice. Addressing entrenched inequalities, arrogant perceptions, and stereotypes is likely to be a gradual and partial process, but an epistemology that includes an explanation of the complex roles of ignorance, including invested ignorance has better resources for such a process, than is available from what could be called an old-fashioned epistemology of knowledge collection and transmission.

NOTES

1. Helen Longino defends pluralism for scientific knowledge in Longino, *The Fate of Knowledge*. See also Stephen H. Kellert, Helen E. Longino, and C. Kenneth Waters, *Scientific Pluralism* (Minneapolis: University of Minnesota Press, 2006), especially vii–xxix. Lorraine Code defends pluralism for everyday, human knowers: "Yet a storied epistemology neither assumes that there is a single, 'true' story, nor that the implications of a story can be read off its surface." Code, *Rhetorical Spaces*, 156.

2. I don't see these as mutually exclusive, this is more a difference in emphasis than a difference in kind.

3. See Longino, *The Fate of Knowledge*. See also Lorraine Code, "Advocacy, Negotiation, and the Politics of Unknowing," *Southern Journal of Philosophy* 66 (2008): 32–51. In this paper, Code examines different attitudes to and uses of evidence in a revision of health care systems in Tanzania.

4. Lorraine Code makes a similar point in identifying "reciprocal effects" between epistemology and developmental psychology. *Ecological Thinking*, 130.

5. See, for example, Bergin, "Testimony, epistemic difference, and privilege."

6. See, for example, Genevieve Lloyd, *The Man of Reason: "Male" and "Female" in Western Philosophy* (Minneapolis: The University of Minnesota Press, 1993); Michele Le Doeuff, *The Philosophical Imaginary*, trans. C. Gordon (Stanford, CA: Stanford University Press, 1989).

7. See, for example, Janice Moulton, "A Paradigm of Philosophy: The Adversary Method," *Discovering Reality*, ed. S. Harding and M. B. Hintikka (Hingham, MA: D. Reidel, 1993), 149–64; Phyllis Rooney "Philosophy, Adversarial Argumentation, and Embattled Reason," *Informal Logic* 30, no. 3 (2010): 203–34.

8. Likewise, as Code has pointed out, it is deeply suspect to assume that peoples with affiliation to "traditional" systems have an irrational aversion to western healthcare. Sometimes western healthcare systems are badly set up and delivered, and it is those factors, not local resistance, that explains a failure to improve health outcomes. See Code, "Advocacy, Negotiation, and the Politics of Unknowing," especially 40–41.

9. The blood related cases arise, for instance, from Hmong beliefs. For the story of a Hmong child with epilepsy and clinical culture clashes see A. Fadiman, *The Spirit Catches you and you Fall Down* (New York: Farrar, Straus and Giroux, 1998). The concern about surgery is a Navajo belief. See L. Alvord *The Scalpel and the Silver Bear* (New York: Bantam, 1999), especially 150–56.

10. Increasingly, people from indigenous communities are representing themselves: Linda Smith both criticises the way that western, or European, research has been aligned with colonialist practice and philosophy and presents an indigenous programme for research projects and priorities, which is emerging from the Maori people of New Zealand. Smith, *Colonizing Methodologies*, 183–95. See also Alvord, *The Scalpel and the Silver Bear*; and the essays in Michele Grossman, ed., *Blacklines: Contemporary Critical Writing by Indigenous Australians* (Melbourne: Melbourne University Press, 2003).

11. A comprehensive discussion of this point can be found in A. Agrawal, "Indigenous and Scientific Knowledge: Some Critical Comments," *Indigenous Knowledge and Development Monitor* 3, no. 3 (1995): 1–5.

12. Grethel Aguilar, "Access to genetic resources and protection of traditional knowledge in the territories of indigenous peoples," *Environmental Science and Policy* 4 (2001): 241–56.

13. . B. Hallen and J. O. Sodipo, *Knowledge, Belief and Witchcraft: Analytic Experiments in African Philosophy* (Stanford: Stanford University Press, 1997), 5.

14. Kant, "What is Enlightenment?" in *Foundations of the Metaphysics of Morals: and What is Enlightenment*, trans. L. White Beck (New York: Macmillan, 1990), 85.

15. Frederique Apffel-Marglin and PRATEC, ed., *The Spirit of Regeneration: Andean culture confronting Western notions of development* (London and New York: Zed Books, 1998), 26.

16. Apffel-Marglin problematizes the description of indigenous relationships with the world as knowledge: "There is no simple act of knowing, for such knowledge acquiring activity presupposes that there is something to be known, irrespective of who knows it." Apffel-Marglin, *The Spirit of Regeneration*, 40. I prefer to revise the conceptions of knowledge in order that such relationships can clearly be included as part of knowledge. A similar position is defended by John O. Browder, "Redemptive Communities: Indigenous Knowledge, Colonist Farming Systems, and Conservation of Tropical Forests," *Agriculture and Human Values* 12, no. 1 (1995), 17–31. Browder suggests that indigenous and colonist knowledge and land use practices be viewed as continuous rather than dichotomous.

17. Apffel-Marglin, *The Spirit of Regeneration*, 33. The words are credited to "a Bolivian peasant."

18. Alvord, *The Scalpel and the Silver Bear*, 112.

19. Alvord, *The Scalpel and the Silver Bear*, 121.

20. Alvord, *The Scalpel and the Silver Bear*, 120.

21. Alvord, *The Scalpel and the Silver Bear*, 127.

22. For a strong criticism of evidence-based medicine see M. Goldenberg, "On evidence and evidence-based medicine: Lessons from the philosophy of science," *Social Science and Medicine* 62, no. 11 (2006): 2621–2632.

23. Julie Stone, "Ethical issues in complementary and alternative medicine," *Complementary Therapies in Medicine* 8 (2000): 210.

24. Edwin Hettinger, "Justifying Intellectual Property," *Philosophy and Public Affairs* 18, no. 1 (1989): 48.

25. Joseph W. Githaiga, "Intellectual Property Law and the Protection of Indigenous Folklore and Knowledge," *E Law - Murdoch University Electronic Journal of Law* 5, no. 2 (1998): 2.

26. Aguilar, "Access to Genetic Resources," 250.

27. Like "bioprospecting" this term refers to the collection of biological specimens and particularly genetic material (even from people as in the Human Genome Diversity Project), from indigenous groups for use by Western scientists in various biotechnology projects. "Piracy" carries the implication of stealing, and emphasises the unscrupulous attitudes and exploitative practices that have been characteristic of some pharmaceutical companies. For example, the patenting of agricultural plants such as the "Enola" bean has allowed a US company to sue the Mexican bean exporters whose communities were the sources for the original seeds from which the patented variety was developed. See "Mexican Bean Biopiracy," Rural Advancement Foundation International News, accessed 23 January 2011, http://www.etcgroup.org/en/node/339. Once a research corporation has patented material sourced from an indigenous community, they acquire exclusive rights to market the resultant products.

28. Joseph Githaiga reports one such case: "In Australia, the Western Australian government has licensed Amrad, a pharmaceutical company, to develop an anti-AIDS drug from the Smoke-bush plant which was traditionally used by Aboriginal peoples for medicinal purposes. Amrad has obtained a global license to develop the patent from the United States National Cancer Institute. Should the project be successful, the WA government will receive royalties in excess of $100 million by the year 2002. No provision, however, has been made for any remuneration of the Aboriginal people who first discovered the medicinal properties of the drug." Githaiga, "Intellectual Property Law," 8. The case of the San people and the Hoodia plant is another well known example.

29. "Biotech firms form alliance to fight off possible TRIPS amendments," GRAIN BIO/IPR/7, accessed 10 January 2006, http://www.grain.org/bio-ipr/?id=463#.

30. "Biotech firms form alliance."

31. C. Quiroz, "Biodiversity, Indigenous Knowledge, Gender and Intellectual Property Rights," *Indigenous Knowledge and Development Monitor* 2, no. 3 (1994): 1–2.

32. I am not claiming here that that such a model accurately describes all scientific activity, just that the discovery model aligns with the view of scientific knowledge as the paradigm of knowledge.

33. Jane Duran, "Feminist Epistemology and Social Epistemics," *Social Epistemology* 17, no. 1 (2003): 53.

34. I argued for this in Cynthia Townley, "Towards an Epistemology of Ignorance," *Hypatia* 21, no. 3 (2006): 37–55.

35. J. Whipps, "Jane Addams's Social Thought," 120.

36. Shannon Sullivan, "Reciprocal Relations between Races: Jane Addams's Ambiguous Legacy," *Transactions of the Charles S. Pierce Society* 39, no. 11 (2003): 49.

37. Marilyn Frye, *The Politics of Reality*, 118.

38. Mills, *The Racial Contract*, 11–18.

39. Code, "The Power of Ignorance," 214.

40. Frye, *Politics of Reality*, 120. The example is taken from a story by Sherley Anne Williams, "Meditations on History," in *Midnight Birds: Stories of Contemporary Black Women Writers*, ed. Mary Helen Washington (New York: Anchor Doubleday, 1980).

41. The example also shows the double face of ignorance—the interviewer's ignorance both denies the slave's capacities and allows the space for her to use them. Knowledge can also both enable what people do, and restrict it, because the ordering of what is known tends to limit attention to other possibilities. This structure shows why ignorance and knowledge can have good and bad aspects from the strategic side.

42. Compare Edward Craig's distinction between sources of information and informants. Craig, *Knowledge and the State of Nature*.

43. Robin Dillon, "Kant on Arrogance and Self-Respect," in *Setting the Moral Compass: Essays by Women Philosophers*, ed. Cheshire Calhoun (New York: Oxford University Press, 2004), 192.

44. This might appear somewhat at odds with Dillon's claim that "even though women can exhibit characteristics that would make it appropriate to call them arrogant, the epithet is rarely applied," since arrogance is self ascribed, for example, collectively in terms of "white solipsism" (Spelman) or individually (Lugones). See Dillon, "Kant on Arrogance," 192; L. Spelman, *Inessential Woman* (Boston: Beacon Press, 1988); Lugones, "Hispaneando y Lesbiando." Nevertheless, calling white solipsism a form of arrogance is, I think, compatible with Dillon's analysis because, whereas in society in general, women don't have an illegitimate share of power and authority, in the context of academic feminism, some (white, middle class, heterosexual) women are privileged relative to others. One might be privileged along one dimension, not on others, so the label of arrogance will be self or other-ascribed in some cases, but elsewhere, or from another direction, the label might be "hostile," "aggressive," or "uppity."

45. An epistemophiliac will see dogmatism as a vice. One dedicated to knowledge will avoid hasty dismissal of others' views and insensitivity to evidence. The point is that epistemophilia can make it harder to recognize dogmatism. But dogmatism is not the only form of epistemic arrogance. One can be arrogant in thinking oneself entitled to acquisition of information, and thus may risk appropriative attitudes, and treating others merely as sources of knowledge rather than agents with their own epistemic considerations including discretion and discrimination. Collecting body parts, funerary items, and sacred objects in order to study them can have this form of arrogance, and arguably, the refusal by museums to return acquired objects to their original owners can continue to manifest arrogance.

46. For example, this obligation and entitlement is characterised as bringing the community closer to the goal of believing all and only truths in Hall and Johnson's account discussed earlier.

47. Maria Lugones, "Playfuless, 'World'-travelling, and Loving Perception," *Hypatia* 2, no. 2 (1987): 18.

48. Code, "The Power of Ignorance," 213–30.

49. Code, "The Power of Ignorance," 217.

50. See, for example, lists by Zagzebski, *Virtues of the Mind*, 179–85; and by James A. Montmarquet, *Epistemic Virtue and Doxastic Responsibility* (Lanham, Maryland: Rowman & Littlefield Publishers, Inc., 1993).

51. Addelson, *Moral Passages*, especially 160–82.

52. Code, "The Power of Ignorance," 224.

53. Code, "The Power of Ignorance," 213.

54. These are the words of Gabrielle Souchon, a seventeenth century French philosopher, quoted in Michele Le Doeuff, *The Sex of Knowing* (New York: Routledge, 2003), 36; quoted in Code, "The Power of Ignorance," 233.

55. Fricker, "Epistemic Injustice," 154–73; see also Townley, "Trust and the Curse of Cassandra," 105–12. Similar damage can occur in abusive relationships which don't conform to group-based patterns of oppression.

56. Rolin, "Gender and Trust," 112.

57. Andy Smith, "For All Those who were Indian in a Former Life," accessed December 27, 2010, http://ishgooda.org/racial/fem1.htm.

Conclusion

I have argued that simple ignorance should not be ignored or devalued in an account of knowledge. While advocating a revisionary epistemology, this work in fact leaves much of traditional epistemology intact, although as a partial, not complete account. Knowledge remains an important element within a plurality of values. Other values derive from the quality and sustainability of the epistemic community, the patterns of participations of its members, its openness to critical reflection, and the range of virtues expressed within the community; for example, those opposed to arrogance as well as to dogmatism. Analyses and norms that refer to knowledge or truth-conduciveness remain part of the theoretical landscape, but neither epistemic practice nor epistemology focus exclusively on these veritistic values. Rather, diverse values interrelate in complicated ways that agents have to navigate, and that theorists have to consider.

The book as a whole approaches epistemology within the framework of virtue theory, and starts from the centrality of interdependence, rather than from an individualist account. Such a reorientation is no longer unusual especially in the context of feminist approaches to epistemology. More radically, this approach resists and revises the common assumption that everything important to epistemology concerns knowledge to the exclusion of ignorance. This revising of the epistemological landscape brings greater clarity about the relationships between epistemic and other interpersonal practices.

Superficially, this approach may seem to conflate or confuse epistemology and ethics. It seems clear to me, although I have not emphasized this in the present work, that sufficient contrast remains between the domains for them to be understood as distinct approaches, even though in theory (as in practice) the concerns of each have significant overlap. Knowledge is important to ethics both because it is involved in identifying contexts where virtuous action is called for and because there is some need to know what one is doing in order to act. However, the same degree of epistemic competence is necessary for effective moral or immoral action, and epistemic excellence seems as distinct from moral virtue as is aesthetic excellence. So the domains need not be conflated on an account that emphasizes interdependence—the sphere of knowledge-related activity and dependence remains distinct.

An ignorance friendly epistemology offers a clear model of how the virtues of epistemic cooperation extend beyond the mere exchange of content, to the rules and norms of the space of reason: the maintenance of standards of justification, rules and norms of evidence and the like. Likewise the scope and limits of epistemic authority, and its impact on social issues, including political and moral matters, and the potential of epistemic authority to be corrupted by invested ignorance has been illuminated. I have argued that recognizing the complex and sometimes positive roles of ignorance can help to explain epistemic practice. Admittedly, a full account of epistemic authority and deference requires considerably more analysis than has been developed here. Nevertheless, the opening of this area is a significant expansion of epistemic concerns to include forms of ignorance. Most significant is the shift of emphasis away from increasing knowledge to questions central to human practice, including an emphasis on the community in which epistemic interactions occur, with the distinct perspective that a focus on ignorance allows. A focus on ignorance also reveals how much epistemology matters for practical concerns. A philosophical account of epistemic agency can contribute to understanding the characteristics needed by information workers and informed citizens, in addition to the ways these are developed, maintained, and cultivated throughout diverse communities. Democratic participation requires an informed and reflective citizenry capable of following and participating in debate on matters of local, national, and global importance. While philosophical analyses operate at a general and abstract level, they yield conclusions relevant to a variety of applications in education, communication, and research. How do we learn and teach about recognition and evaluation of expertise? How do we respond to testimonial claims by members of indigenous groups about the significance of sacred sites when the underlying grounds are presented as "secret business"? How do diverse attitudes to authority and tradition interact within complex communities and how do responsible epistemic agents deal with pluralism? The present account shows how taking ignorance seriously can help us to engage with such questions. Standard accounts, due to their exclusive appeals to knowledge collection and promotion, do not do so well in the face of these questions.

I have argued against knowledge as the exclusive epistemic value and against the assumption that independent acquisition of knowledge is superior to interdependence. I hope that this work shows at least that these claims need to be argued for, not just assumed. Ignorance should not be presumed epistemic failure nor ignored by epistemologists.

Bibliography

Addelson, Kathryn P. *Moral Passages.* New York; London: Routledge, 1994.

Adler, Jonathan E. "Testimony, Trust, Knowing." *The Journal of Philosophy* 91(5) (1994): 264–75.

Adler, Jonathan E. "Epistemic Dependence, Diversity of Ideas and a Value of Intellectual Vices." *The Proceedings of the Twentieth World Congress of Philosophy, Vol. III: Philosophy of Education.* Edited by D. M. Steiner. Columbia: Bowling Green University Philosophical Documentation Center, 1999.

Agrawal, A. "Indigenous and Scientific Knowledge: Some Critical Comments." *Indigenous Knowledge and Development Monitor* 3(3) (1995): 1–5.

Aguilar, Grethel. "Access to genetic resources and protection of traditional knowledge in the territories of indigenous peoples." *Environmental Science and Policy* 4 (2001): 241–56.

Allen, A. L. *Uneasy Access.* Totowa, New Jersey: Rowman and Littlefield, 1988.

Alvord, L. *The Scalpel and the Silver Bear.* New York: Bantam, 1999.

Apffel-Marglin, Frederique and PRATEC, ed. *The Spirit of Regeneration: Andean Culture Confronting Western Notions of Development.* London and New York: Zed Books, 1998.

Audi, Robert. "The Place of Testimony in the Fabric of Knowledge and Justification." *American Philosophical Quarterly* 34 (4) (1997): 405–22.

Austin, J. L. "Other Minds." In *J. L. Austin: Philosophical Papers*, 2nd ed, edited by J. O. Urmson and G. J. Warnock, 76-116. Oxford: Clarendon Press, 1970.

Axtell, Guy. "Recent Work on Virtue Epistemology." *American Philosophical Quarterly* 34(1) (1997): 1–26.

Axtell, Guy. "Expanding Epistemology: A Responsibilist Approach." *Philosophical Papers* 37(1) (2008): 51–87.

Bailey, Alison. "Strategic Ignorance." In *Race and Epistemologies of Ignorance,* edited by Shannon Sullivan and Nancy Tuana, 77-94. Albany: State University of New York Press, 2007.

Becker, Lawrence C. "Trust as Noncognitive Security about Motives." *Ethics* 107 (1996): 43-61.

Bergin, Lisa A. "Testimony, Epistemic Difference, and Privilege: How Feminist Epistemology Can Improve Our Understanding of the Communication of Knowledge." *Social Epistemology* 16(3) (2002): 197–213.

Braaten, Jane, "Towards a Feminist Reassessment of Intellectual Virtue." *Hypatia* 5 (3) (1990): 1–14.

Browder, John O. "Redemptive Communities: Indigenous Knowledge, Colonist Farming Systems, and Conservation of Tropical Forests." *Agriculture and Human Values* 12(1) (1995), 17–31.

Bedau, Hugo A. "Paternalism." In *The Oxford Companion to Philosophy*, edited by T. Honder-ich, 647. Oxford: Oxford University Press, 1995.

Burkhart, Brian Y. "What Coyote and Thales Can Teach Us." In *American Indian Thought*, edited by Anne Waters, 15-26. Oxford: Blackwell Publishing, 2004.

Calhoun, Cheshire. "Cognitive Emotions?" In *What is an Emotion? Classical Readings in Philosophical Psychology*, edited by C. Calhoun and R. C. Solomon, 327-342. New York and Oxford: Oxford University Press, 1984.

Campbell, Nancy D. "Reconstructing Science and Technology Studies: Views from Feminist Standpoint Theory." *Frontiers: A Journal of Women Studies* 30(1) (2009): 1–29.

Campbell, Nancy D. and Mary Margaret Fonow, ed. *Frontiers: A Journal of Women Studies (Special Issue) Knowledge that Matters: Feminist Epistemology, Methodology and Science Studies* 30:1 (2009).

Code, Lorraine. *Epistemic Responsibility*. Hanover and London: University Press of New England, 1987.

Code, Lorraine. *What Can She Know?* Ithaca and London: Cornell University Press, 1991.

Code, Lorraine. *Rhetorical Spaces: Essays on Gendered Locations*. New York: Routledge, 1995.

Code, Lorraine. *Ecological Thinking*. Oxford: Oxford University Press, 2006.

Code, Lorraine. "The Power of Ignorance." In *Race and Epistemologies of Ignorance*, edited by Shannon Sullivan and Nancy Tuana, 213-230. Albany: State University of New York Press, 2007.

Code, Lorraine. "Advocacy, Negotiation, and the Politics of Unknowing." *Southern Journal of Philosophy* 66 (2008): 32–51.

Craig, Edward. *Knowledge and the State of Nature: An Essay in Conceptual Synthesis*. Oxford: Oxford University Press, 1990.

Dalmiya, Vrinda and Linda Alcoff. "Are 'Old Wives' Tales' Justified?" In *Feminist Epistemologies*, edited by L. Alcoff and E. Potter, 217–45. New York and London: Routledge, 1993.

Dana, Jason and George Loewenstein. "A Social Science Perspective on Gifts to Physicians from Industry." *Journal of the American Medical Association* 290 (2) (2003): 252–55.

de Sousa, Ronald. *The Rationality of Emotion* (Cambridge, MA: MIT Press, 1987).

Dickens, Charles. *Hard Times*. Harmondsworth: Penguin, 1995.

Dillon, Robin. "Kant on Arrogance and Self-Respect." In *Setting the Moral Compass: Essays by Women Philosophers*, edited by Cheshire Calhoun, 191–216. New York: Oxford University Press, 2004.

Driver, Julia. "The Virtues of Ignorance." *The Journal of Philosophy* 86 (7) (1989): 373–84.

Duran, Jane. "Feminist Epistemology and Social Epistemics." *Social Epistemology* 17(1) (2003): 45–54.

Fadiman, A. *The Spirit Catches You and You Fall Down*. New York: Farrar, Strauss and Giroux, 1998.

Foucault, Michel. *The Archaeology of Knowledge*, trans. A. M. Sheridan Smith. New York: Routledge, 2002.

Fricker, Elizabeth. "The Epistemology of Testimony." *The Aristotelian Society, Supplementary Volume* 61 (1987): 57–84.

Fricker, Elizabeth. "Against Gullibility." In *Knowing From Words*, edited by B. K. Matilal and A. Chakrabarti, 125–62. Dordrecht: Kluwer, 1994.

Fricker, Miranda. "Rational Authority and Social Power: Towards a Truly Social Epistemology." *Proceedings of the Aristotelian Society* 98(2) (1998): 159–77.

Fricker, Miranda. "Epistemic Injustice and a Role for Virtue in the Politics of Knowing." *Metaphilosophy* 34(1/2) (2003): 154–73.

Fricker, Miranda. "Powerlessness and Social Interpretation." *Episteme: A Journal of Social Epistemology* 3(1-2) (2006): 96–108.

Fricker, Miranda. *Epistemic Injustice: Power and the Ethics of Knowing*. New York: Oxford University Press, 2007.

Frye, Marilyn. *The Politics of Reality: Essays in Feminist Theory*. Trumansberg, NY: The Crossing Press, 1983.

Githaiga, Joseph W. "Intellectual Property Law and the Protection of Indigenous Folklore and Knowledge." *eLaw Journal: Murdoch University Electronic Journal of Law* 5(2) (1998): URL http://www.murdoch.edu.au/elaw/issues/v5n2/githaiga52.html.

Goldenberg, M. "On evidence and evidence-based medicine: Lessons from the philosophy of science." *Social Science and Medicine* 62 (11) (2006): 2621–632.

Goldman, Alvin. "Epistemic Paternalism: Communication Control in Law and Society." *The Journal of Philosophy* 88(3) (1991): 113–31.

Goldman, Alvin. "Epistemic Folkways and Scientific Epistemology." in *Readings in Philosophy and Cognitive Science,* edited by A. Goldman, 95–116. Cambridge, Massachusetts: MIT Press, 1993.

Goldman, Alvin. *Knowledge in a Social World.* Oxford: Clarendon Press, 1999.

Goonatilake, S. "Transfer Systems in Science and Technology and Indigenous Intellectual Initiatives." *Philosophy and Social Action* 13(1-4) (1987): 9–25.

Graham, Peter. "Testimony, Agency and Entitlement." Paper presented at the Southern California Philosophy Conference, Irvine, California, September 27, 2001.

Graham, P. J. "Transferring Knowledge." *NOUS* 34(1) (2000): 131–52.

Grain. "Biotech firms form alliance to fight off possible TRIPS amendments," GRAIN BIO/IPR/7, accessed January 10, 2006, http://www.grain.org/bio-ipr/?id=463#.

Grasswick, H. and M. O. Webb. "Feminist epistemology as social epistemology." *Social Epistemology* 16(3) (2002): 185–96.

Michele Grossman, ed. *Blacklines: Contemporary Critical Writing by Indigenous Australians.* Melbourne: Melbourne University Press, 2003.

Hall, Richard J. and Charles R. Johnson. "The Epistemic Duty to Seek More Evidence." *American Philosophical Quarterly* 35(2) (1998): 129–39.

Hallen, B. and J. O. Sodipo. *Knowledge, Belief and Witchcraft: Analytic Experiments in African Philosophy.* Stanford: Stanford University Press, 1997.

Hanrahan, R. and L. Antony. "Because I Said So: Toward a Feminist Theory of Authority." *Hypatia* 20(4) (2005): 59–79.

Hardin, Robert. "Trustworthiness." *Ethics* 107 (1996): 26–42.

Harding, Sandra. "Rethinking Standpoint Epistemology." In *Feminist Epistemologies,* edited by L. Alcoff and E. Potter, 49-82. New York and London: Routledge, 1993.

Harding, Sandra. "Two Influential Theories of Ignorance and Philosophy's Interests in Ignoring Them." *Hypatia* 21(3) (2006): 20–36.

Hettinger, Edwin. "Justifying Intellectual Property." *Philosophy and Public Affairs* 18(1) (1989): 31–52.

hooks, bell. *Feminist Theory from Margin to Center.* Boston: South End Press, 1984.

Hookway, Christopher. "Some Varieties of Epistemic Injustice." *Episteme* 7 (2010): 151–63.

Hume, David. *A Treatise of Human Nature,* 2nd ed., edited by P. Nidditch. Oxford: Clarendon Press, 1978. Original publication 1739.

Jones, Karen. "Trust as an Affective Attitude." *Ethics* 107 (1996): 4–25.

Kant, Immanuel. "What is Enlightenment?" In *Foundations of the Metaphysics of Morals, and What is Enlightenment?,* 2nd ed., translated by L. White Beck. New York: Macmillan, 1990.

Kellert, Stephen H., Helen E. Longino, and C. Kenneth Waters, ed. *Scientific Pluralism.* Minneapolis: University of Minnesota Press, 2006.

Kvanvig, Jonathan. *The Intellectual Virtues and the Life of the Mind.* Savage: Rowman and Littlefield, 1992.

Lahno, Bernd. "On the Emotional Character of Trust." *Ethical Theory and Moral Practice* 4 (2001): 171–89.

Le Doeuff, Michele. *The Philosophical Imaginary,* translated by C. Gordon. Stanford, CA: Stanford University Press, 1989.

Lloyd, Genevieve. *The Man of Reason: "Male" and "Female" in Western Philosophy.* Minneapolis: The University of Minnesota Press, 1993.

Longino, Helen. *The Fate of Knowledge.* Princeton and Oxford: Princeton University Press, 2002.

Lugones, Maria. "Playfulness, 'World'-Travelling, and Loving Perception." *Hypatia* 2 (2) (1987): 3–19.

Lugones, Maria. "Hispaneando y Lesbiando: On Sarah Hoagland's *Lesbian Ethics.*" *Hypatia* 5 (3) (1990): 138–46.

Meiland, Jack. "What Ought We To Believe? or The Ethics of Belief Revisited." *American Philosophical Quarterly* 17 (1980): 15–24.

Mills, Charles. *The Racial Contract.* Ithaca, NY: Cornell University Press, 1997.

Moulton, Janice. "A Paradigm of Philosophy: The Adversary Method." In *Discovering Reality*, edited by S. Harding and M. B. Hintikka, 149–64. Hingham, MA: D. Riedel Publishing, 1993.

Nyquist Potter, Nancy. *How Can I Be Trusted?: A Virtue Theory of Trustworthiness.* Maryland: Rowman and Littlefield, 2002.

Peirce, C. S. "How to Make Our Ideas Clear." In *Charles S. Peirce: Selected Writings*, edited by Philip Wiener, 113–36. New York: Dover Publications, 1958. First published 1878.

Peirce, C. S. "Some Consequences of Four Incapacities." In *Charles S. Peirce: Selected Writings*, edited by Philip Wiener, 39–72. New York, Dover Publications, 1958. First published 1868.

Pettit, Philip. "The Cunning of Trust." *Philosophy and Public Affairs* 24(3) (1995): 202–25.

Quiroz, C. "Biodiversity, Indigenous Knowledge, Gender and Intellectual Property Rights," *Indigenous Knowledge and Development Monitor* 2 (3) (1994): http://www.iss.nl/ikdm/ ikdm/ikdm/2-3/articles/quiroz.html

Rawls, John. *A Theory of Justice.* London: Oxford University Press, 1973.

Spender, Dale. *Invisible Women: The Schooling Scandal.* London: Writers and Readers, 1982.

Rolin, Kristina. "Gender and Trust in Science." *Hypatia* 17(4) (2002): 95–118.

Rooney, Phyllis. "Philosophy, Adversarial Argumentation, and Embattled Reason." *Informal Logic* 30(3) (2010): 203–34.

Rural Advancement Foundation International. "Mexican Bean Biopiracy," Rural Advancement Foundation International News, accessed January 23, 2011, http://www.etcgroup.org/en/ node/339

Schiebinger, Londa. *Plants and Empire: Colonial Bioprospecting in the Atlantic World.* Cambridge, MA: Harvard University Press, 2004.

Smith, Andy. "For All Those who were Indian in a Former Life," accessed December 27, 2010, http://ishgooda.org/racial/fem1.htm. Originally published in *Women of Power*, Winter 1991.

Smith, Linda T. *Decolonizing Methodologies: Research and Indigenous Peoples.* London: Zed Books, 1999.

Solomon, Robert C. and Fernando Flores. *Building Trust: In Business, Politics, Relationships, and Life.* Oxford: Oxford University Press, 2003.

Spelman, L. *Inessential Woman.* Boston: Beacon Press, 1988.

Stone, Julie. "Ethical issues in complementary and alternative medicine." *Complementary Therapies in Medicine* 8 (2000): 207–13.

Sullivan, Shannon. "Reciprocal Relations between Races: Jane Addams's Ambiguous Legacy." *Transactions of the Charles S. Peirce Society* 39(11) (2003): 43–60.

Townley, Cynthia. "Trust and the Curse of Cassandra: An exploration of the value of trust." *Philosophy in the Contemporary World* 10(2) (2003): 105–12.

Townley, Cynthia. "Towards an Epistemology of Ignorance." *Hypatia* 21(3) (2006): 37–55.

Tuana, Nancy. "The Speculum of Ignorance: The Women's Health Movement and Epistemologies of Ignorance." *Hypatia* 21(3) (2006): 1–19.

Webb, M. O. "Why I Know About As Much As You: A Reply to Hardwig." *The Journal of Philosophy* 90(5) (1993): 260–70.

Whipps, J. "Jane Addams's Social Thought as a Model for a Pragmatist-Feminist Communitarianism." *Hypatia* 19(2) (2004): 118–33.

Williams, Patricia J. *The Alchemy of Race and Rights: Diary of a Law Professor.* Cambridge, MA: Harvard University Press, 1991.

Williams, Sherley Ann. "Meditations on History." In *Midnight Birds, Stories of Contemporary Black Women Writers*, edited by Mary Helen Washington, 200–248. New York: Anchor Doubleday, 1980.

Young, Iris M. *Justice and the Politics of Difference.* Princeton: Princeton University Press, 1990.

Zagzebski, Linda. *Virtues of the Mind*. Cambridge: Cambridge University Press, 1996.
Zagzebski, Linda. "Responses." *Philosophy and Phenomenological Research* 60(1) (2000): 207–19.
Zagzebski. Linda. "Epistemic Trust." *Philosophy in the Contemporary World* 10(2) (2003): 113–17.

Index

Addelson, Kathryn Pyne, ix, 73, 75, 76, 82–83, 85n48
Adler, Jonathan, 26, 83n6
agency (epistemic), 9, 13, 35, 42, 44, 48, 50, 52n31, 30, 70, 101, 114; responsible, xiv, 24, 25; and community, 4, 13, 18; recognition of, 10, 44, 53n64, 61, 76, 78
Aguilar, Grethel, 91, 96
Alcoff, Linda, 74
Alvord, Lori, 92, 93
alternative and complementary medicine, 90
analytic epistemology, x, 2, 99
Apffel-Marglin, Frederique, 92, 109n16
arrogance, 55, 79, 85n55, 88, 89, 99, 101–102, 103, 106, 106–107, 110n44, 113
Audi, Robert, 37
Austin, J. L., 52n39
authority, xii, xviii, xx, 2, 8, 50, 51n6, 53n60, 66, 70, 76, 92, 94, 100, 114; and dependence, 5–6; and empathy, 78–83; and expertise, 59–61, 64, 70, 71, 73, 73–74, 75, 84n15; institutionalization, 45, 55, 58; and paternalism, 62–63, 64, 65. *See also* expertise, paternalism; and respect, 13, 18, 41; responsible, 9, 10, 11, 75, 76, 82–83; as social, xxiin28, 25, 26, 43, 45–46, 48, 49, 82, 101, 102, 110n44; and trust, 4, 35, 41, 45, 46

autonomy, 3, 4–5, 8, 10–11; autonomy obsession, 2, 4
Axtell, Guy, xxin3

Becker, Lawrence, 50n5
Bergin, Lisa, 18, 20n12
betrayal, xiv, 23, 30, 32, 33, 34, 36
bioprospecting, xiii, 92, 109n27
Braaten, Jane, xiv, 13–15, 21n31, 42, 48, 49, 53n56, 58, 85n50, 102, 104
Browder, John, 109n16
Burkhart, Brian, xxin2

Calhoun, Cheshire, 31, 51n24
Cassandra, 23, 44–45, 48, 53n64, 58, 82
Code, Lorraine, xiii, xxin9, 2, 19n4, 21n27, 44, 78, 85n50, 100, 102, 103, 105, 108n1
collective, xiv, xv, 12, 46, 58, 73, 75, 76, 82, 85n50, 96. *See also* community (epistemic)
community (epistemic), xiv, xv, xvii, xix, 1, 2, 14–15, 75, 76; and epistemic justice, 48, 58, 78, 106; inclusiveness of, xv, 13, 42; need for adequate account of, 1, 2–3, 7, 13, 16, 17, 18, 20n19, 23, 25, 48, 70, 113; and scientific communities, 2, 42, 57; and trust, 26, 34, 35, 35–36, 41, 44, 47, 60, 80; vices and virtues of, 13, 14–15, 16, 20n23, 21n30, 24, 50, 57, 83n6, 87, 95,

Fricker, Miranda, x, 20n15, 23, 24, 46, 47, 48, 49, 50, 52n32, 58, 78, 82, 84n16, 102, 104
Frye, Marilyn, 55, 100–101, 102, 103

gender, xi, xx, xxiin27, 25, 39, 46, 47, 56–57, 88, 98, 106
Githaiga, Joseph, 96, 109n28
Goldman, Alvin, xii, xxin5, 16, 20n14, 21n26, 24, 26, 50n4, 61–62, 63–64, 64–65, 65, 66–67, 68, 68, 69–70, 71, 83, 84n11, 85n33
Graham, Peter, 20n16, 84n10
Grasswick, H. M. (and M. O. Webb), xxiin26
gullibility, 23, 26, 31, 34, 35, 36, 40, 45, 51n19

Hall, Richard (and Charles Johnson), 16–17, 17–18, 51n12, 62, 70, 84n31, 110n46
Hanrahan, R. (and Antony), 53n60, 83n2, 84n15
Harding, Sandra, xi, 64, 74, 76, 85n50
Hettinger, Edwin, 95
hooks, bell, 82
Hookway, Christopher, 20n21
Hume, David, 6, 41, 43

ignorance: ascribed, xi, 79, 88, 106, 107; in empathic knowledge. *See* empathy; authority and empathy; exclusionary, xx, 105; invested, x–xi, xiii, xx, 25, 47, 51n10, 55, 56, 57, 59, 79, 82, 88, 88, 94, 95, 100–101, 104, 105, 107, 114; as methodological, xvi, 24; problematic; ignorance invested; arrogance; selective, 56, 59; and trust, 24, 25–26, 27, 34–35, 41; types of, ix, x–xi, xvii, xx, 55, 88; veil of, xvi. *See also* arrogance, gender, race
imperialism, 78, 85n51
independence (epistemic). *See* dependence
interdependence (epistemic). *See* dependence, trust
individualism, xx, xxiin26, 2, 8, 12, 16, 17, 19n4, 21n28, 62, 67, 68, 70, 83, 88–89, 113

institutional epistemic dependence. *See* authority, division of epistemic labor, expertise
intellectual property rights (IPR), 90, 95, 95–96, 96, 97, 99
intellectual virtue, xiv, xv, xvii, 12, 13, 14–15, 42, 44, 53n56, 85n50. *See also* epistemic: epistemic virtue, feminist intellectual virtues

Johnson, Charles (and Richard Hall). *See* Hall, Richard
Jones, Karen, 31, 31, 32, 34, 39, 40, 52n29, 53n54

knowledge: as atomistic, 34, 37, 95; collection view, xiii, xix, 35, 45, 61, 76, 92, 93, 98, 99, 107, 114; conduciveness, xii, xiii, 3, 89, 98, 101; as socially constructed, 15, 73, 74, 76; excessive love of. *See* epistemophilia; and power, 46, 48, 55, 58, 62, 62–63, 74, 76, 77–78, 79, 80, 81, 83, 84n29, 85n48, 88, 96, 99, 102, 106, 110n44; production, xv, 57, 59, 73, 74, 76; as unified whole, xvi, 98; pluralism: pluralism and knowledge
Kvanvig, Jonathan, 4, 4, 10, 10–11, 18, 19n6, 21n46

Lahno, Berndt, 31, 39, 40, 42, 51n24, 53n51
Longino, Helen, 71, 108n1
Lugones, Maria, xiv, 102, 103

Meiland, Jack, 27
midwives, 74, 82
Mill, James, 103–105, 107
Mills, Charles, x, 100

norms of civility, xiv, 42, 82, 76, 102, 104, 106

objectivity, xvii, 74, 76, 79, 82, 85n50
oppression, xi, xx, xxin1, 24, 25, 45, 48, 82, 86n56, 88, 106, 111n55. *See also* subordination

Peirce, Charles Sanders, xiv, xvi

About the Author

Cynthia Townley is lecturer of philosophy at Macquarie University in Sydney, Australia.